Penny Croucher

The ultimate guide
to a unique city

Further information on the Internet.

Bibliografische Information der Deutschen Nationalbibliothek
Die Deutsche Nationalbibliothek verzeichnet diese Publikation in der Deutschen Nationalbibliografie; detaillierte bibliografische Daten sind im Internet über http://dnb.d-nb.de abrufbar.

Alle Rechte vorbehalten.
Dieses Werk, einschließlich aller seiner Teile, ist urheberrechtlich geschützt. Jede Verwertung außerhalb der engen Grenzen des Urheberrechtsgesetzes ist ohne Zustimmung des Verlages unzulässig und strafbar. Das gilt insbesondere für Vervielfältigungen, Übersetzungen, Mikroverfilmungen, Verfilmungen und die Einspeicherung und Verarbeitung auf DVDs, CD-ROMs, CDs, Videos, in weiteren elektronischen Systemen sowie für Internet-Plattformen.

© berlin edition im be.bra verlag GmbH
Berlin-Brandenburg, 2012
KulturBrauerei Haus 2
Schönhauser Allee 37, 10435 Berlin
post@bebraverlag.de
Umschlag: Ansichtssache, Berlin
Innengestaltung: Friedrich, Berlin
Schrift: Garamond condensed 10/11,6 pt
Druck und Bindung: TPC
ISBN 978-3-8148-0190-2

www.bebraverlag.de

Contents

1.	The Berlin Feeling	5
2.	Easy Riding	9
3.	City Centre Sights	21
4.	Cool Collections	53
5.	Small Worlds	77
6.	The Outer Edges	101
7.	Stage and Screen	115
8.	Late Nightlife	131
9.	Café Society	143
10.	Buy, Buy Berlin	161
11.	The Berlin Calendar	175
12.	Special Dossier:	
	Jewish Berlin	179
	Hitler's Berlin	191
	Divided Berlin	203
	The Berlin Wall	211
	Berlin Timeline	220
	Acknowledgements	222
	The Author	223
	Index of photographs	223

The Berlin Feeling

Berlin is a city that conjures up strong images: Prussians and Kaisers, an outrageous nightlife, Nazi rallies, bombed-out buildings, Soviet tanks, the Wall and the May Day riots. It has risen again from a chaos of ruins, survived 40 years of division and reinvented itself as the capital of a unified Germany. Now the message is "Berlin is poor but sexy", a shabby-chic city ravaged by graffiti, a place where creativity can flourish, but whose reputation remains dubious. Its past evokes feelings of horror and fascination and the present is a potent mix of glamour and seediness. The cultural scene is diverse and dynamic and the variety of cityscape and landscape is breathtaking.

When Mark Twain came to live in Berlin in 1890 he was struck by its beauty and size. He wrote: "It is a new city, the newest I have ever seen ... The next factor that strikes one is the spaciousness, the roominess of the city." Over two hundred years later 21st century Berlin is a fledgling metropolis once again. It is also a vibrant patchwork of boroughs and districts – small worlds that are at the heart of Berlin's survival and revival.

My own love affair with Berlin started during the Cold War, over a weekend in August 1974. I travelled there by British Military train through the 'enemy territory' of East Germany. Our carriages were locked and armed guards stood by the doors. Left on my own for a day, I tried to get a feel for the city. First stop was the Brandenburg Gate with the bizarre sight of the Berlin Wall blocking it off and slicing the city in half. The Reichstag stood just inside West Berlin; a gloomy, blackened façade, stranded on a battle front.

On the barren wasteland of Potsdamer Platz there were tour buses clustered around the makeshift souvenir stands and together with all the coach trippers I climbed the viewing platform to stare across the bleak expanse of the death strip into East Berlin. At Checkpoint Charlie there were still more tourists, taking photos of the border crossing and filing past the escape stories in the museum.

Televison Tower, Mitte

Kaiser-Wilhelm-Gedächtnis-Kirche, Charlottenburg

In the afternoon the gleaming splendour of Charlottenburg Palace and its manicured gardens seemed surreal in contrast to the greyness of the morning. There was a lively street market in full swing across the road and the sun shone on the pavement cafés. West Berlin now seemed a light-hearted, happy place. A night out on Kurfürstendamm was a raucous affair, even if the illuminated church ruin seemed to stand in judgment on all the nightclubs and neon signs. I had caught the 'Cabaret' mood and knew I wanted to return to this unique city. The streets were wide and tree-lined and there were sparkling lakes and deep green forests on the way in and out of the city centre. Yet behind the Wall there was another Berlin, unknown territory harbouring faded Prussian and Imperial glory, just waiting to be discovered.

Ten years later I got my wish and came to live in West Berlin for two years. My job as feature writer for the British newspaper was a dream assignment; being paid to write about a city I was hooked on. I had free access to East Berlin and was able to explore the suburbs as well as the historic centre. Here were cobbled streets full of pot-holes and crumbling façades that bore the scars of war. I also worked as a tourist guide, accompanying coach loads of visitors to see the main sights of both West and East Berlin. My script included sensational details about Hitler's Berlin and the

Potsdamer Platz, Tiergarten/Mitte

Communist enemy behind the Berlin Wall. But I found I didn't want to exaggerate the city's dark side. I wanted people to understand it, not fear it. The Berliners I met had a sardonic sense of humour that had seen them through hard times and their city had become mine too.

When I had to move on, in my suitcase was a souvenir given to me by a Berlin friend. It was a small metal bear with one foot in Berlin. Marlene Dietrich famously sang that she still had a suitcase in Berlin, but it was 30 years before she returned to her native city after leaving for Hollywood in 1930. My suitcase has gone back and forth countless times over the years. I was there to see the fall of the Wall and have followed every pang of the German capital's rebirth.

Berlin is still recreating itself, a place where the possibilities are endless and anyone can join the party. In 1800 German novelist Jean Paul described Berlin as, 'more a part of the world than a city'. Today this is truer than ever. If you can embrace the clash of cultures that is the lifeblood of the city, then you will find it endlessly fascinating. That is the Berlin feeling.

The Berlin Feeling

Easy Riding

Getting around Berlin is a breeze. For pedestrians the pavements are gloriously wide and there are cycle paths almost everywhere. On foot or by bike you can see everything close up and breathe in plenty of 'Berliner Luft', the unique Berlin air that is said to be as addictive as cocaine or alcohol. You may also become hooked on the Berlin public transport network mainly run by the BVG (Berliner Verkehrsgesellschaft – Berlin Transport Company). It is simple to use and the sights and sounds will add new dimensions to your impressions of the capital. Many of the stations on the U-Bahn (underground) and the S-Bahn (urban railway) have a nostalgic feel. The elevated sections of the railway give you a great view of the cityscape and some of the double-decker buses take you past the main tourist attractions. The trams only run in East Berlin and are an essential part of the Berlin experience. Outside the city centre, there are also a few ferry services.

Tickets can be used on all forms of transport. There are three zones; Zone A is the city centre within the S-Bahn's circle line 'Ringbahn'; Zone B is the rest of Berlin surrounding the circle line and you only need a ticket that includes Zone C if you travel outside the city limits, for example to Potsdam or Oranienburg. It is vital to 'validate' your ticket the first time you use it. This involves getting it stamped with the date and time in machines which are on station platforms and on every bus and tram. If caught travelling without a valid ticket you'll be subject to a fine. Ticket inspectors don't wear uniforms and often look more like buskers or punks than officials.

There are ticket machines on station platforms, at some bus stops and on all trams. Only larger stations have ticket offices, but tickets can also be bought at the airport, at tourist information offices and some newsagents – just look out for the 'BVG' sign. On buses you can buy tickets from the driver. The basic 'Einzelfahrschein' ticket is valid for two hours for any journey and there is a discount if you buy 4 tickets at a time. There is also a cheaper 'Kurzstrecke' ticket for short trips of up to 6 bus or tram stops and 3 stops on the U- or S-Bahn. If you are making more than three journeys on the same day, a 'Tageskarte' (day travel pass) is better value. There are also several special visitor tickets. These include a group day ticket for up to five people,

U-Bahn at Tempelhofer Ufer, Kreuzberg

a 48 hour or 72 hour 'WelcomeCard' which comes with a coupon booklet and a 'CityTourCard' with even more discounts and a combined museum pass. The BVG's website has an excellent English link with all the details and timetables at **www.bvg.de**.

Surfing the network
The U-Bahn
Most of Berlin's underground lines are only just sub-surface because of the sandy Berlin soil. The word U-bahn is short for Untergrundbahn (underground rail) and pronounced 'ooo-barn'. The trains are yellow and the logo is a white 'U' on a blue background. There are nine lines on the Berlin network, originally built in two major phases. The first phase (1902–1913) was the construction of the 'Kleinprofil' network which includes the east-west lines U1 to U4. The next phase, completed in 1930, was the 'Großprofil' network that established the first north-south lines. The trains on lines U5 to U9 are wider and taller and some stations are of vast proportions.

Architect Alfred Grenander designed over 70 of Berlin's pre-war U-Bahn stations and some have been wonderfully restored. Wittenberg Platz and Rathaus Schöneberg are more like monuments and Klosterstraße has fin-de-

U-Bahn station Rathaus Schöneberg

siècle charm. Mohrenstraße was rebuilt after the war using the marble taken from Hitler's former Reich Chancellery. On the U3 line, don't miss the vaulted Heidelberger Platz and the historic railway paintings at Breitenbachplatz. The elevated track of the historic U1 crosses the Spree over the iconic Oberbaumbrücke and passes through multi-cultural Kreuzberg on its journey westwards. Most of the 13 stations still evoke the atmosphere of pre-war Berlin and when you look up into the iron girders and then along the curved rail as a small yellow train approaches, you might catch that Berlin feeling.

Grenander's stations on the U8 line are much larger, with sequences of columns and ceiling lights. Hermannplatz is like an U-Bahn cathedral and was the first to be equipped with escalators. But the biggest of all the U-Bahn stations is Alexanderplatz, completely redesigned and expanded in the 1920s when this area was the vibrant hub of the city centre. The post-war phase of Berlin U-Bahn construction consisted mainly of extending existing lines. Over 40 of these stations in West Berlin were designed by Rainer Rümmler. Some tunnel walls feature historic scenes associated with the area and in the 1980s Rümmler's stations became rather lavish and garish. During Berlin's division many of the U-Bahn stations in East Berlin were Geisterbahnhöfe (ghost stations) where trains ran from one side of West Berlin to the other without stopping. These eerie places, guarded by the shadowy figures of East

German soldiers, have now been brought back to life and given a facelift. The most recent addition to the U-Bahn network is line U55 between Hauptbahnhof and Brandenburger Tor. The new Bundestag station has a futuristic feel with its steel minimalism and soaring ceilings.

The S-Bahn

A ride on the Berlin S-Bahn is more than a journey – it synchronises you with the city's rhythm. In summer it whisks you quickly to the lakes and forests and the snow in winter adds a layer of nostalgia to the old cobbled platforms. The term S-Bahn is an abbreviation of 'Stadtschnellbahn', meaning 'urban rapid rail'. Its symbol is a white 'S' on a green circle and the trains are traditionally red and mustard coloured. Lines run from the suburbs on to three main routes through the city centre. The Stadtbahn is the east-west route and links all the main railway stations. The Nord-Süd-Bahn runs north-south and the Ringbahn encircles the city centre. All S-Bahn lines are numbered and and platform signs show the destination and important stations en route.

S-Bahn history

Electrification of the S-Bahn was completed in 1929 and the next project was a tunnel to join the two lines that ran into the city centre from the north and south. This tunnel, known as the Nord-Süd-Bahn, became a matter of prestige for the Nazis. The first section from the north to Unter den Linden opened for the Berlin Olympics in 1936 and the second section, running through Potsdamer Platz, opened in October 1939. Many sections of the S-Bahn were closed during the war and the Nord-Süd-Bahn tunnel was flooded on 2nd May 1945 by retreating SS troops during the final Battle for Berlin.

After the war the S-Bahn service in the western sectors of Berlin continued to be operated by the Deutsche Reichsbahn, as were all rail services in East Germany, whereas in West Germany they were now operated by the Bundesbahn. This meant that during the Cold War the Berlin S-Bahn soon became a victim of hostilities. The S-Bahn service stopped at Friedrichstraße in both directions and this station was divided into two separate areas and became one of the crossing points for visitors to East Berlin. Service on the Nord-Süd-Bahn was operated for western passengers only. It passed through a short stretch under East Berlin territory and trains didn't stop at these stations – they too became ghost stations. The Ringbahn only ran between the stations which went through East Berlin.

S-Bahn station Savignyplatz, Charlottenburg

West Berliners vented their frustration at the building of the Wall by boycotting the East Berlin operated S-Bahn and the BVG began providing new bus services as an alternative. The West Berlin employees of the S-Bahn went on strike and the western portion of the S-Bahn was shut down in September 1980. At the same time, services on the S-Bahn in East Berlin were increased and new lines were built as housing projects expanded eastward from the city centre. The BVG later took over the responsibility for operating S-Bahn services in West Berlin and a limited service was restored. Since reunification a great deal of money and effort has been put into restoring the entire S-Bahn network which is now operated by Deutsche Bahn (German Rail).

Scenic city route

The stretch of S-Bahn track between Savignyplatz in West Berlin and Alexanderplatz in East Berlin is a must for visitors. The raised tracks first take you between the backs of tall buildings variously 'decorated' with murals, adverts and graffiti. The next stop is Zoologischer Garten, West Berlin's central station, a vast metal cage which was frequented by the homeless and drug-addicted during the city's division. From here the S-Bahn line winds

Tram at Hackescher Markt, Mitte

past Berlin Zoo and on to Tiergarten station, crossing over Berlin's east-west axis. The route continues through the city's main park and the blocks of flats in the 'Hansaviertel', an area rebuilt as an architectural competition in the late 1950s. To the right is a view of the Siegessäule (Victory Column).

After Bellevue the S-Bahn crosses the Spree and draws into Berlin's new Hauptbahnhof. This giant temple of glass and steel pulsates with the movement of people and trains on dozens of levels. The next stretch gives a wonderful panorama of the new government district, the Reichstag and the cluster of skyscrapers at Potsdamer Platz. Then Friedrichstraße station ushers in historic East Berlin. The greyness of this shed-like station still seems to reek of Cold War days and there is an atmospheric walkway under the iron girders to Schiffbauerdamm. On the station forecourt to the left, now dwarfed by an office tower, is the oddly shaped 'Tränenpalast' (Palace of Tears). This was the former GDR transit building, the scene of many sad farewells during the city's division. The S-Bahn glides onwards between majestic museums and into the intricate brickwork and round leaded-light windows of Hackescher Markt station. From here to Alexanderplatz the cityscape is filled with communist-style blocks of flats and offices and the television tower rears up to the right and dominates the skyline.

The Buses

For tourists the most important bus routes are the 100 and 200 which run between Zoologischer Garten and Alexanderplatz. There are great views of the city's main sights from the top of these double-deckers. Bus 100 takes you through the Tiergarten and stops at the Reichstag before it continues down Unter den Linden. Bus 200 calls at the Kulturforum and Potsdamer Platz en route to Alexanderplatz.

Several 'Metrobuses' are also useful for tourists and many of them operate a 24 hour service. The M29 from Hermannplatz in Neukölln to Grunewald in Charlottenburg runs through Kreuzberg past Checkpoint Charlie and along the full length of the Kurfürstendamm, calling at the Kulturforum and Potsdamer Platz. Metro Buses M41 and M85 both run between the Hauptbahnhof and Potsdamer Platz. The M85 passes the Brandenburger Tor and the Holocaust memorial – the only form of public transport to do so.

The Trams

Berlin's tram network, one of the oldest and largest in the world, is now concentrated in former East Berlin. There are 22 tram lines and nine of them run all night. Horse-drawn trams were introduced in 1865 and in 1881 Berlin opened the world's first electric tram line. By 1930 the network had 90 different lines, although many disappeared when the city was being restructured by Nazi planners. War-time bombing damaged the tram lines and in April 1945 the system collapsed during the final Battle for Berlin. After 1949 trams could no longer travel through the city centre and by 1961 West Berlin had only 18 lines left. The erection of the Berlin Wall was the final blow and West Berlin replaced their remaining trams with buses. Today several of the Metrobus routes follow former tram lines.

Soviet Moscow with its tram-free avenues was the role model for East Berlin's transport planning and many tram lines closed in the 1950s and 1960s. But in the late 1970s some new sections were built to connect the new socialist housing estates of Marzahn, Hohenschönhausen and Hellersdorf to the city's tram network. Tram routes may not follow the main tourist trail but riding a 'Straßenbahn' is a great experience as you rumble and bend your way through the streets of East Berlin. The yellow carriages full of light glide through the day and late into the night, creating a moving showcase of Berlin faces. The M1 tram trip is a magical mystery tour past some of the best street views of East Berlin from Pankow to the Pergamon Museum.

Taxi at Gendarmenmarkt, Mitte

Taxis

A cab is sometimes the quickest and easiest option. The cream-coloured Berlin taxis are reasonably priced and there always seem to be plenty of them. In the city centre it is quite easy to hail a taxi and there are taxi ranks in all the main areas. You don't have to take the taxi at the front of the queue but can select the one you want and there are lots of women drivers. On all buses and trams, after 10pm you can ask the driver to call a taxi to meet you at your stop.

Tours

Berlin has a huge range of sightseeing tours on offer. There are hundreds of companies offering bus, boat, bike and walking tours and they can be booked online, at any tourist information office or from your hotel. You can also just turn up at the Brandenburg Gate at 11am for a 'free' walking tour in English around the main sights – the excellent young guides will just expect a discretionary tip. Tours with a difference include an independent audio tour, a Segway tour or a veteran bus tour on the 'Zille Express'. A nostalgic but more active experience is the 'Trabi Safari', a tour of the city sights from behind the wheel of a GDR Trabant. For breathtaking aerial views of the whole city there is the Berlin HiFlyer. This 'Welt Ballon' is one of the big-

HiFlyer, Mitte

gest helium balloons in the world and has become quite a trademark of the capital. From its launch pad near Checkpoint Charlie it silently ascends to about 150 metres and there you hover for about 15 minutes enjoying the amazing 360° panorama.

Berlin also has a vast system of waterways, more canal bridges than Venice and an infinite choice of boat trips. There are double-deckers full of tourists steaming past the graffiti-splattered banks of the Spree in the city centre and canal trips through former border areas and industrial backwaters. Out on the lakes there are excursions to suit everyone or you can hire a boat and take to the waters on your own.

The following websites cover most possibilities:

www.air-service-berlin.de
www.berlinonbike.de
www.citysegwaytours.com/berlin
www.city-sightseeing.com
www.fahrradtouren-berlin.de
www.FreeBerlinTours.de
www.inberlin.de
www.insidertour.com
www.newberlintours.com
www.radundtouren.de
www.reederei-riedel.de
www.segtour-berlin.de
www.stadt-im-ohr.de
www.stattreisenberlin.de
www.sternundkreis.de
www.trabi-safari.de

Easy Riding

City Centre Sights

Berlin is a unique showcase for visitors. In many respects it still feels like two cities separated by the huge Tiergarten Park, but as well as East Berlin and West Berlin there is now a new 'Central Berlin' built on land which was flattened in the war and then further laid waste when the Berlin Wall cut through the heart of the city. Here, time stood still and created large empty spaces where no one lived. When Berlin was reunited it was transformed into one vast building site and although the construction and reconstruction continues, the sense of space has been preserved, enhancing the effect of the architecture. Buildings are set apart, individually or in set-piece ensembles like pictures at an exhibition and because Berlin is not a high-rise city, on a clear day you can see forever. This guide to the main sights of Berlin divides the city into East, West and Central Berlin and includes the best vantage points for heavenly views.

East Berlin

East Berlin contains the historic centre of the German capital, largely created by the Prussian King, Frederick the Great (Friedrich II), almost three centuries ago. It was locked behind the Iron Curtain for 40 years and its rebirth after the war reflected the political ideals of its communist rulers. Since reunification renovation work and new development has been relentless, with a replica of the Berliner Stadtschloss (Berlin City Palace) due for completion in 2019 and many other projects underway.

Brandenburger Tor

The Brandenburg Gate is one of Europe's most famous landmarks and the last remaining Berlin city gate. It stands proudly in the middle of Pariser Platz, straddling the main ceremonial avenue of the German capital. Crowned by its Quadriga sculpture, a four-horsed chariot driven by the Goddess of Victory, it has been a focal point in Berlin's history. Rulers and statesmen, military parades and demonstrations have all felt compelled to march

The Brandenburg Gate

through it. It was modelled on the gateway to the Acropolis in Athens and constructed by Karl Gottfried Langhans in 1793. At that time, only the Prussian royal family was allowed to pass through the central archway.

The Brandenburg Gate was originally commissioned to represent peace, but it has since seen turbulent times. After defeating the Prussians in 1806, Napoleon's Army marched through it into Berlin and took the Quadriga back to France. It was returned in 1814 following the Prussian occupation of Paris. When the Nazis came to power in 1933 they used the Brandenburg Gate for their torchlight parades and from 1961 to 1989 it was masked by the Berlin Wall. Since the historic night of 9th November 1989 it has become a symbol of reconciliation again and the focal point of all the celebrations to mark the fall of the Wall. There was a period when vehicles could drive under the Brandenburg Gate, but now the whole area is for pedestrians only. There is a tourist office in the south wing and a 'Raum der Stille' (Room of Silence) in the north wing for a few minutes of quiet contemplation.

Pariser Platz

This square, laid out between 1732 and 1734 by Frederick the Great's court architect Georg Wenzeslaus von Knobelsdorff, was given its current name after the Prussian troops captured Paris. By 1850 it was the grandest square in Berlin surrounded by buildings in largely classical style and it remained unchanged for almost a century. Although heavily bombed in the war, several buildings were in reparable condition, including the Hotel Adlon, but in the weeks following capitulation the hotel burned down during a raucous party held by celebrating Soviet army officers. The square became wasteland and eventually part of the death zone dividing the city. In 1990 work started on reconstructing Pariser Platz as a fine urban space complete with cobblestones, fountains and trees. The embassies moved back, Hotel Adlon and the Akademie der Künste (Academy of Arts) were reinstated and rich international firms were encouraged to build round the square. Under the rules of reconstruction, height had to be restricted to 22 metres, buildings had to be properly defined against the skyline and stone cladding was to be used as far as possible.

The new Hotel Adlon dominates the south-east side of Pariser Platz and is a copy of the original building. Michael Jackson famously stayed here in 2002 and dangled his child from the balcony of his room. Next door the Akademie der Künste incorporates the ruins of the old Academy of Arts behind a vast expanse of windows. The DZ Bank at 3 Pariser Platz combines the clean lines of Prussian architecture with an oval glass roof. In the southwest corner of Pariser Platz is the heavily guarded and rather nondescript American Embassy. The French Embassy on the north side of the square is in contrast an elegant new building with colonnades and tall windows similar to its predecessor. To its left the Berlin headquarters of the Dresdner Bank has a plain sandstone façade but an exciting interior design and next door the Palais am Pariser Platz features shops and cafés around a shaded courtyard. Adjoining the north wing of the Brandenburg Gate is Haus Liebermann, a faithful replica of the pre-war building on the same site, named after the eminent Jewish artist, Max Liebermann, who lived here from 1892 until his death in 1935. In 1933, watching Nazi SA troops march through the Brandenburg Gate, he famously said: "I cannot possibly eat as much as I would like to puke out."

Unter den Linden

Pariser Platz leads into Unter den Linden, a majestic avenue, one mile long and 200 feet wide, planted with four rows of lime trees and dating back to the beginning of Berlin's rise to fame as capital of Brandenburg. Originally a hunting path, in 1647 the Great Elector, Friedrich Wilhelm I, turned it into a ceremonial avenue from his Stadtschloss to the Tiergarten. The first buildings were houses and inns at the western end, followed by the Zeughaus (Armoury) and other official buildings at the eastern end. In 1724 Frederick the Great commissioned Knobesldorff to extend and enhance it. At the beginning of the 19th century the most famous of German classical architects, Karl-Friedrich Schinkel designed the Neue Wache (New Guardhouse) and the Schlossbrücke (Palace Bridge) with its fabulous white marble statues depicting the life of a Greek warrior. It was during this century that Unter den Linden became the Berliners' favourite promenade. The houses in the western part were superseded by cafés, wine bars and shops and by the beginning of the 20th century there were also huge banks, large businesses and luxury hotels in the ornate style of the 'Gründerzeit', the era of the Kaisers towards the end of the 19th century. The corner of Unter den Linden and Friedrichstraße was then one of the busiest junctions in the world.

Unter den Linden has witnessed many historic events. The French Army under Napoleon rolled over its stones and in the 1848 Revolution it was the scene of violent clashes and demonstrations. After the wars of 1866 and 1870–71 the Prussian Armies celebrated their victories with parades and in August 1914 fervent German nationalists gathered here to mark the advent of the First World War. Four years later revolutionary workers, soldiers and sailors marched up the avenue to the Stadtschloss to cheer Karl Liebknecht as he proclaimed the first German Socialist Republic. Hitler used it for many of his parades and Bebelplatz was the site of the notorious Nazi burning of the books in 1933. During the war Unter den Linden tried hard to retain its image of light-hearted pleasure but by 1945 most of its buildings were reduced to a pile of rubble. The Soviets insisted that the new buildings at the western end still had to conform in height to the 'Linden Statute' (1880) so that the avenue retained its architectural appeal, but during Berlin's division the atmosphere of excitement and life disappeared. The shops and cafés were half-dead, policemen stood on every corner and the ceremonial goose-stepping march of East German soldiers changing the guard at the Neue Wache had a chilling effect.

Now Unter den Linden is bustling with people again. There is a well-known Marlene Dietrich song that promises that as long as the lime trees still blossom on Unter den Linden, "Berlin will always be Berlin". Shops, restaurants and hotels have sprung up between Pariser Platz and Friedrichstraße, the historic buildings of Prussian and Imperial Berlin have undergone restoration and modern architecture has created new highlights. The

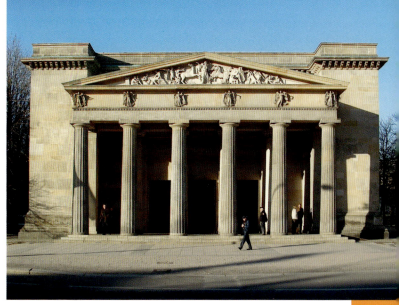

New Guardhouse, Unter den Linden, Mitte

first building to stand out on the right hand side is the imposing Russian Embassy (63–65 Unter den Linden). This vast edifice was built in the Stalinist-classicist style on the site of the old embassy, an 18th century Rococo palace. The buildings on the left side of Unter den Linden, opposite Hotel Adlon, are currently occupied by global brands that can afford the rents. After Wilhelmstraße comes the Hungarian Embassy (75–76), Madame Tussauds (70) and the new glass-fronted Forum Willy Brandt Berlin (62–68). The next building of interest is the Zollernhof (36–38), for many years home of the FDJ (GDR communist youth organisation). The historic façade has been retained, but the German television company ZDF has transformed the interior into their Berlin headquarters, neatly arranged around a courtyard complex of shops and cafés.

On the other side of Unter den Linden, behind the modernist ensemble of buildings directly on Unter den Linden, is the Komische Oper (Comic Opera), one of Berlin's three opera houses. The 'Haus der Schweiz' on the corner of Friedrichstraße is the only remaining building from the Nazi era, opposite the site of the legendary Café Kranzler, which moved to West Berlin during the 1950s when the owner saw which way the political wind was blowing. Past Charlottenstraße on the right is the Deutsche Guggenheim, an

City Centre Sights

experimental art museum in a 1920s Deutsche Bank building. The rows of lime trees now come to an end and you are confronted with Frederick the Great himself. This grand bronze statue, in the middle of Unter den Linden is of 'Old Fritz' on his favourite horse, wearing coronation robes, a tri-cornered hat and top boots. It is wonderfully ornate and worth a closer look. Historians say that it took nearly 70 years to determine the final plan for the equestrian statue of the much-revered king. Construction of the statue began in 1839 under the watchful eye of its creator, Christian Daniel Rauch.

On Frederick the Great's right is Bebelplatz, the focal point of the Forum Fridericianum, his great project to create a cultured city centre echoing the elegance and splendour of Ancient Rome. The original square was called Opernplatz but was renamed in 1947 after August Bebel, a founder of the Social Democratic Party of Germany. In the middle of the empty cobbled space is the underground memorial to the Nazi burning of the books (page 200). Bebelplatz is flanked by two superb buildings; the richly ornamented Staatsoper built by Knobelsdorff in 1741–43 as Europe's first free-standing opera house and the former State Library, now the Law Faculty of the Humboldt University, nicknamed 'die Kommode' (chest of drawers) by the Berliners. Behind the Staatsoper is St Hedwigs-Kathedrale, also designed by Knobelsdorff and modelled on the Pantheon in Rome. Frederick the Great commissioned this cathedral to appease the Catholics in Berlin after conquering Silesia. It has been rebuilt with a modern interior. Next to it, facing the square, is an imposing imperial building. Originally owned by the Dresdner Bank, it became the headquarters of the East German state bank and has now been converted into the stylish Hotel de Rome. To the left of the Staatsoper is the Opernpalais, once a palace for the Hohenzollern princesses. It is connected to the Kronprinzenpalais by an arched bridge added in 1810. This neo-classical palace was built for the heirs to the Hohenzollern throne and after the Kaiser's abdication it became an art museum. It is an exact copy of the original, reconstructed in the late 1960s and used in the GDR era to receive foreign dignitaries. The German reunification agreement was signed here on 31st August 1990.

Opposite Bebelplatz, on the other side of Unter den Linden, is the main building of the Humboldt-Universität, Berlin's oldest university, founded in 1810 on the initiative of educational reformer, academic and statesman Wilhelm von Humboldt, whose younger brother Alexander was the famous German naturalist. Twenty-nine Nobel Prize winners were educated here, including Albert Einstein. Other famous students include Karl Marx and Otto

Humboldt-Universität, Bebelplatz, Mitte

von Bismarck. The Staatsbibliothek at 8 Unter den Linden is the main State Library, an imposing neo-baroque building (1908–13) with a beautiful inner courtyard. The Neue Wache (New Guardhouse) on the other side of the University was Schinkel's first royal commission and is the main German memorial for all victims of war. An enlarged reproduction of the Pietà sculpture by Käthe Kollwitz, who lost a son in the First World War and a grandson in the Second World War, conveys the message perfectly.

Behind the Neue Wache are two further reconstructions of neo-classical style buildings. The Palais am Festungsgraben is hired out by the Federal State of Berlin to host various events and the Maxim Gorki Theater was formerly the Singakademie, a major Berlin concert hall in the 19th century. Paganini, Schumann, and Brahms all performed here and on 11th March 1829, a 21 year old Felix Mendelssohn conducted his famous revival of Bach's St Matthew Passion. The oldest building on Unter den Linden is the Deutsches Historisches Museum, Germany's largest history museum. It started life as the Zeughaus, an armoury for the Prussian military and later developed into a State Army Museum. Badly damaged in the war, it was rebuilt over a period of several years and has now been beautifully restored and a new extension added. The muted pink exterior with its fabulous sculptures adorning the roof is stunning.

City Centre Sights

The Lustgarten, Mitte

Museumsinsel Island of Museums

Unter den Linden ends at Schinkel's elegant Schloßbrücke which leads regally on to Museumsinsel. In 1999 this island of museums in the middle of the River Spree was declared a UNESCO Heritage Site. The five internationally-renowned museums form a perfect architectural grouping and are described in detail in 'Cool Collections'. In front of the Altes Museum is the Lustgarten (pleasure garden) created in 1573 for the Hohenzollern Prussian royal family. In the 18th century Friedrich Wilhelm I turned it into a military parade ground and in the 1930s it was used for Nazi parades and rallies. It was re-landscaped in 2000 according to original plans.

The Berliner Dom (Berlin Cathedral) is Berlin's largest and most important Protestant church. It was first built in 1465 as a parish church on the Spree and the 'old' Cathedral was designed by Knobelsdorff and constructed between 1747 and 1750 under Frederick the Great. From 1817 to 1822 Schinkel redesigned it, but retained its stylistic similarity to the high-renaissance baroque architecture of St. Peter's in Rome. When Wilhelm II became Kaiser in 1888 he ordered its demolition and the construction of a much larger Berliner Dom began. It was heavily damaged during the war and cycles of restoration continued until 2006. The main impact of its ornate interior lies in the obvious attempt to forge state with religion. The organ is a master-

Berliner Dom, Mitte

piece and the ninety Hohenzollern family tombs in the crypt make an impressive sight. But the highlight is the 114 metre dome. The inside is decorated with golden mosaics and from the outside there are exclusive views of the historic centre of East Berlin. The 270 steps are quite wide and well worth the climb.

Opposite the Berliner Dom is Schloßplatz, where the mighty Stadtschloss once stood. In 1950 the GDR government demolished its bombed ruins in spite of West German protests. This royal palace had been the principal residence of the Hohenzollern Kings of Prussia (1701–1918) and the German Emperors from (1871–1918) and dominated Berlin's city centre. The only façade retained by the GDR featured the balcony from which Karl Liebknecht proclaimed the Socialist Republic on 9th November 1918 and in 1964 it was incorporated into the new Staatsrat (State Parliament) building on part of the site of the former Stadtschloss. Today this building houses the European School of Management and Technology. From 1976 until 2006 the Palast der Republik occupied the space between Schlossplatz and the Lustgarten. This people's palace had copper-coloured mirrored windows and contained the GDR 'parliament' as well as two auditoria, art galleries, a theatre, restaurants, a bowling alley and a discothèque. The Berliners had several nicknames for it, including 'Palazzo Prozzo' ('protzen' means 'to show off').

City Centre Sights

Gendarmenmarkt, Mitte

Amid some controversy, it was finally demolished in 2008 and the site has been cleared to await construction of the 'Berlin Palace-Humboldt-Forum'. You can learn all about this exciting project in the 'Humboldt-Box', a huge, futuristic blue metal structure alongside the building site. It incorporates an exhibition area with a wonderful model of historic Berlin as well as the exciting plans for the Humboldt-Forum itself, due for completion in 2019.
| www.humboldt-box.com

Gendarmenmarkt

The Gendarmenmarkt is among the most beautiful squares in Europe. The wonderfully composed buildings with their graceful statues seem to imprint themselves indelibly on the skyline and the cobblestones and street lamps lend the square an air of nostalgia. On warm evenings you can sit outside and enjoy the violin music of the street musician. In July it is the stage for the Open Air classics concerts and in December there is a traditional Christmas market. It started life as a market place and its name is derived from the Regiment Gens d'Armes who had their stables here from 1736 to 1773. The three splendid buildings on the Gendarmenmarkt are the 'twin cathedrals' and the Konzerthaus (Concert hall), built by Schinkel in 1821 as the Schauspielhaus (playhouse). When post-war reconstruction finished in 1984 it reopened as a concert hall. In front of it the statue of poet, philosopher and dramatist Friedrich Schiller radiates the great worth of 19th century German culture.

The Französischer Dom (French Cathedral) and Deutscher Dom (German Cathedral) were built as churches rather than cathedrals, despite their names. The Französischer Dom on the right is an adornment to the Französische Friedrichstadtkirche behind it. This church was built between 1701 and 1705 by French Huguenots who had sought refuge in Protestant Berlin. Services are still held here and it is also used for organ recitals and classical concerts. The 'dome' part contains a Huguenot museum and a viewing platform which provides a perfect vantage point from which to appreciate the Italian inspired 'Forum Fridericianum'. The Deutscher Dom was built as the 'Neue Kirche' in 1708 under Elector Friedrich III who had crowned himself King of Prussia and wanted to turn Berlin into a royal residence to rival Versailles. In 1780, inspired by St Paul's Cathedral in London, his grandson Frederick the Great commissioned Carl von Gontard to build a non-functional dome for each of the two churches. The Deutscher Dom was destroyed in 1945 and wasn't fully rebuilt until 1993. It is now a museum of German parliamentary history.

Alexanderplatz

Alexanderplatz – 'Alex' to Berliners – was immortalised by Alfred Döblin in his famous novel 'Berlin Alexanderplatz' (1929) as the hub of 1920s working-class Berlin. Döblin's Alexanderplatz was obliterated in the war, but this square still belongs to the common man and on 4th November 1989 thousands of people congregated here to demonstrate against the GDR regime. It once lay just outside the city gates, served as a cattle market in the Middle Ages and then a military parade square and exercise ground until the mid-19th century. It was named to honour Alexander I, Tsar of Russia, on his visit to Berlin in 1805. Its transformation into a commercial centre began during the second half of the 19th century with the development of the railway and the elevated rails of Alexanderplatz station still sweep along one side of the square.

Its present appearance dates from the re-birth of the East German city centre from 1966 to 1971 when the GDR government tried to compete with West Berlin's attempts at a new high-rise modern city centre. They built the former state-owned Centrum department store (now Galeria Kaufhof), the

Alex shopping arcades (now Alexa shopping mall), the towering Stadt Hotel (now Park Inn Hotel) and the gigantic Fernsehturm (TV Tower) transmitting the confidence of the new communist era. Alexanderplatz is also home to the 'Weltzeituhr' (World Time Clock) a popular meeting place for Berliners and the Brunnen der Völkerfreundschaft (Fountain of International Friendship) which has seen better days. It is overlooked by GDR architect Henselmann's Haus des Lehrers (Teachers' Building) with its bold socialist murals and the Haus des Reisens (Travel Building), a rather ironic name in view of the travel restrictions during GDR times.

In the middle of the large expanse on the other side of the station is the impressive Neptunbrunnen (Neptune Fountain) built in 1891. The Roman god is in the centre surrounded by four women who represent the four main rivers of Prussia. The fountain was removed from its original location on Schloßplatz in 1951 when the royal palace was demolished. Dwarfed by the Fernsehturm is the Marienkirche, dating back to 1270 and originally Roman Catholic. In the 15th century it acquired the tower at the front, in 1539 it became Protestant and in 1790 the tower was crowned with a baroque and neo-gothic dome. It was fully restored after the war and contains many wonderful artworks from the destroyed medieval churches nearby. In the entrance is the 'Totentanz' (Dance of Death) a large fresco painted during the plague epidemics and discovered in 1960 under layers of paint. Outside the church is a large bronze statue of Martin Luther.

Opposite the Marienkirche is the Berliner Rathaus, seat of the Mayor of Berlin and the Berlin Senate. Berliners call it the 'Rotes Rathaus' referring to the building's red brick façade but this has often been an apt description for its political leanings. Built from 1861–69, it is decorated with the 'Stone Chronicle', showing scenes from Berlin's history and in front of it is a sculpture of the citizens of Berlin rebuilding their city. The grand red-carpeted staircase leads up to the Großer Festsaal, a large vaulted gallery now used for special occasions and exhibitions and the Wappensaal (Hall of Arms). Even more stunning is the Säulensaal (Hall of Pillars) with its soaring nine-metre ceiling, brightly painted to resemble Sienna's 'Palazzo Pubblico'. The Rathaus is only open on weekdays and entrance is free.

Heavenly views

At 368 metres (1,207 feet) the Fernsehturm is the tallest structure in Germany and the fourth highest in Europe. Wherever you go in East Berlin its round head seems to peer over the rooftops, bringing a sense of humour to

Berlin panorama

the skyline. When the sun shines on its stainless steel sphere, the reflection appears in the form of a crucifix. This effect was not planned by its atheist architects and Berliners immediately nicknamed the luminous cross 'Die Rache des Papstes' (The Pope's Revenge). Inside the shaft of the Fernsehturm are two lifts that shuttle visitors up to the sphere in 40 seconds. The viewing platform is 204 metres above the ground and visibility can reach 42 kilometres on a clear day. Just above the platform is a restaurant, which rotates once every 30 minutes. The Hotel Park Inn on Alexanderplatz was constructed at the same time as the Fernsehturm. From the 37th floor (125 metres) there are superb views across East Berlin and beyond and in summer there are deckchairs on the roof terrace and an open air lounge. The Park Inn also offers the attraction of 'Base Flying' where participants stun the crowds below by plunging vertically to the ground in a controlled fall.

Marx-Engels-Forum

This public park was created in 1986 on the eastern bank of the Spree. Before the war it was part of the densely populated 'Altstadt' (medieval quarter). This was heavily bombed in 1944/45 and after the war the ruins were cleared but nothing was built to replace them. In the centre of the

Marx-Engels-Forum, Mitte

Marx-Engels-Forum is a paved area with a sculpture consisting of larger-than-life bronze figures of Marx and Engels and behind it a relief wall showing scenes from the history of the German socialist movement. After reunification some Berliners wanted to get rid of the statues and rename the park, but others felt the site had artistic and historical merit and should be preserved. The statues remain and provide a popular photo opportunity for tourists.

Nikolaiviertel and Medieval Berlin

The Nikolaiviertel is a GDR reconstruction of Berlin's oldest quarter. When it was completed in 1987 to celebrate the city's 750th Anniversary, Berlin was still divided and ironically the city's beginnings also consisted of two rival towns, Cölln and Berlin, on either side of the Spree. The most important building here is the 13th century Nikolaikirche. Schinkel carried out restructuring in 1807 and the towers were added from 1876–78. It was deconsecrated and turned into a museum in 1938. The interior has recently been beautifully restored. Another important architectural landmark in the Nikolaiviertel is the Ephraimpalais. This baroque palace, now a museum and gallery, was dismantled in 1935/36 as part of Hitler's street widening

Nikolaiviertel, Mitte

programme, stored in numbered pieces and then rebuilt in 1983. The elegantly curving façade, gilded wrought-iron balconies, famous oval staircase and ceiling by Schlüter on the first floor combine to make it one of Berlin's most exquisite buildings. Two further significant houses, now used as museums, are named after their original owners. The Nicolaihaus dates back to 1674 and the Knoblauchhaus is a reconstruction of a 1760 building. Several medieval-looking inns compete for the title of 'oldest tavern' in Berlin, but to find the earliest authentic traces of Berlin you have to leave the Nikolaiviertel and cross Mühlendamm.

On Jüdenstraße is the massive Altes Stadthaus, built in 1880 as an extension to the main town hall. Behind it on Klosterstraße are the ruins of the Franziskaner Klosterkiche, a medieval early-gothic style church belonging to a Franciscan monastery in Cölln and dating back to 1250. There is also a section of the original 13th century Berlin wall on the corner of Waisenstraße and on the same street, the oldest bar and restaurant in Berlin and survivor of the bombing, 'Zur Letzten Instanz'. Built in 1561 its name means 'at the last judgment' referring to the courthouse nearby. Both Napoleon and Beethoven are said to have dined here, seated next to the 200 year old stove. You can wander back to Klosterstraße station through the graveyard of Parochialkirche (1695), the first reformed church in Berlin.

Hackescher Markt

The final central part of East Berlin spans out from Hackescher Markt station and includes the original Jewish quarters of Berlin, described in detail in 'Jewish Berlin'. It is an area outside the old city walls and before the war parts of it were considered slums. After the war it remained neglected for many years; there were huge gaps where buildings had been bombed and then demolished and those still standing had crumbling blackened façades and were full of bullet holes. Reconstruction work was just starting when the Berlin Wall fell. Now its streets are among the most fascinating and colourful in Berlin. You can discover all the best haunts in 'Small Worlds' and 'Late Nightlife'.

Hackescher Markt was originally laid out as a market square by Frederick the Great in 1750 when Berlin was being expanded to the north and 'Hacke' was the name of the Berlin mayor at the time. The Hackesche Höfe on the corner of Rosenthaler Straße are a wonderful example of the courtyards typical of Berlin's 'Gründerzeit' (1870–1914) which contained a mixture of workshops, multi-storey factories, offices and flats. They were built in the early 1900s and have been beautifully renovated and converted. Hof I (Endellscherhof), designed by the art nouveau artist and architect August Endell, has a cabaret theatre, cinema, bars and restaurants. The remaining seven courtyards contain a mixture of designer shops, galleries and flats.

The Scheunenviertel (Barn Quarter) refers to the neighbourhood east of Rosenthaler Straße and Hackescher Markt up to Rosa-Luxemburg-Platz. Its name derives from the barns erected in 1672 to store hay for the cattle market. Friedrich Wilhelm I required all Berlin Jews to settle here in 1737 and it gradually became poverty-stricken. Before World War I some parts were redeveloped but the Scheunenviertel was rampaged by Nazi Stormtroopers in the 1930s and after the war the whole area fell into neglect. Almost next to the Hackesche Höfe at 39 Rosenthaler Straße is Haus Schwarzenberg. Here the two gloomy courtyards haven't been gentrified and are covered in graffiti and posters. In the first courtyard are three moving Jewish museums and the second courtyard has an arts cinema, a couple of alternative cafés, shops and galleries. The atmosphere of studied anarchy evokes a feeling of the pre-war slums.

Further along Rosenthaler Straße turn left into Sophienstraße, where the buildings date back to the 18th century and have been lovingly restored. The Sophie-Gips-Höfe (three courtyards linking Sophienstraße and Gipsstraße) have an interesting mix of buildings combining an old factory, 19th century Biedermeier houses and contemporary architecture.

Haus Schwarzenberg, Mitte

Across the street is the Sophienkirche, Berlin's only surviving baroque church. Named after Frederick I's third wife, it spreads historic charm through the network of cobbled streets around it, especially when the church bells echo across the old graveyard. Sophienkirche faces Große Hamburger Straße which is in Spandauer Vorstadt, the original centre of Berlin's Jewish cultural and commercial life. This area is often mistakenly included as part of the Scheunenviertel because the Nazis wanted to denigrate Jewish life and equated it with the slum area nearby. There are two architectural highlights in Oranienburger Straße; the restored façade of the Neue Synagoge (described in 'Jewish Berlin') and the 'Postfuhramt', a striking brick building on the corner of Tucholskystraße, built as the depot for Berlin's horse-drawn postal wagons.

West Berlin

Like many big cities, Berlin has a 'west end' traditionally associated with shopping, entertainment and expensive real estate. West Berlin is all these things and more. From 1949 until 1989 it was an island stranded in a sea of communism, but helped by subsidies from the mainland of West Germany it managed to attract both business and tourism and to become a city in its own right.

The Elephant Gate entrance to the Berlin Zoo, Charlottenburg

Bahnhof Zoo Zoo Station

The large railway station of Zoologischer Garten, opened in 1882 and rebuilt by the Nazis is the gateway to West Berlin. It is opposite the main Berlin zoo and only two minutes walk from the Kurfürstendamm, the grand boulevard of West Berlin. When the city was divided the station took on great significance as West Berlin's main rail link with the rest of Western Europe and in the 1970s and 1980s it was notorious as a hangout for drug addicts and young prostitutes. It was the setting for the book and film based on the true story of a teenage heroine addict, 'Christiane F.' and the inspiration for the U2 song 'Zoo Station'.

Kaiser-Wilhelm-Gedächtnis-Kirche
Emperor William Memorial Church

On the night of 18th November 1943 this great church burned down after it was hit by an Allied bomb; all that remained was the broken west tower. Local opposition saved it from demolition and it now stands starkly in the centre of West Berlin as a permanent reminder of the war. Berliners call it "der hohle Zahn" (the hollow tooth). Opened in 1895 by Kaiser Wilhelm II, the church was a symbol of Prussian unity and a mark of honour for his

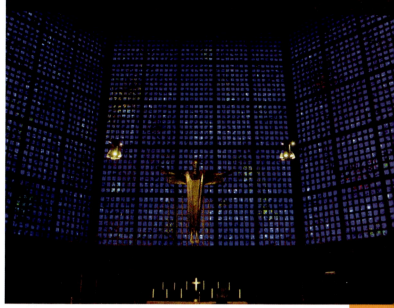
Kaiser-Wilhelm-Gedächtnis-Kirche, Charlottenburg

grandfather, Kaiser Wilhem I. Inside the tower is a Gedenkhalle (Memorial Hall) which documents the history of the church and displays some of the original objects and decorations. In 1961 an octagonal concrete church was built next to it and a freestanding bell tower on the site of the main nave of the destroyed church. Both feature dark blue coloured glass bricks, especially effective by night. The church contains the Stalingrad Madonna, an image of the Virgin Mary drawn by a German soldier in 1942 during the Battle of Stalingrad.

Breitscheidplatz

The Gedächtnis-Kirche stands on Breitscheidplatz. This square was first called Gutenbergplatz after the inventor of the printing press, then three years later renamed Auguste-Viktoria-Platz in honour of the German Empress. In 1947 it was named after Rudolf Breitscheid, a German Social Democrat who died in Buchenwald concentration camp in 1944. Facing the square is the Europa-Center, a 1965 shopping centre regarded as the epitome of modern urban development in post-war West Berlin. It was built on the site of the legendary 'Romanisches Berlin', a meeting place for the intelligentsia in the 1920s, including author Erich Kästner, playwright Bertolt

Brecht and film director Billy Wilder. Russian poets in exile gathered there too and writer Andrei Bely described the atmosphere with the words, 'The Night! Tauentzien! Cocaine!'

On the north side of the Europa-Center is Budapester Straße, best known for its 1950s Filmpalast cinema, once the heart of the Berlin Film Festival. Behind it are the main Berlin Zoo and the Aquarium, both with excellent international reputations. During the allied bombing many of the animals escaped and wandered the streets of Berlin, a surreal experience that also caught U2's imagination. The splendid Elephant Gate entrance to the Zoo is further down Budapester Straße.

Kurfürstendamm

The long grand boulevard referred to by Berliners as the 'Ku'damm' takes its full name from the former Kurfürsten (Electors) of Brandenburg who used it as a bridle-path to their Grunewald hunting lodge. Since the days of the Kaiser its broad pavements have been lined with shops, hotels, theatres, restaurants and street cafés. Tall, black wrought-iron street lamps bow elegantly above the glass display cases introduced by the Nazis and the busy street corners have quaint kiosks and the old-style 'Litfaßsäule', columns advertising all the current shows and concerts. In summer the four rows of magnificent plane trees hide the parked traffic and in winter their branches sparkle with white lights.

After the Prussians defeated the French in 1871, Otto von Bismarck wanted the Kufürstendamm to become Berlin's version of the Champs-Elysées in Paris. It was widened to about 53 meters (174 feet) and the construction of some of the city's most prestigious addresses began. The buildings had ornate façades with columns, gables, towers and huge bay windows and the interiors featured high ceilings and grand entranceways. Over half these magnificent structures were destroyed during the war, but some have been lavishly restored.

Galerie Brusberg (213) gives an idea of the Kurfürstendamm's former neo-classical splendour and 'Iduna-Haus'(59) on the corner of Leibnizstraße is a turreted building with a richly ornamented Art Nouveau façade. A good way of enjoying the Ku'damm sights is to take a double-decker bus as far as Adenauerplatz and back. Many of the apartments that were once home to Berlin's rich and famous are used as offices and the Ku'damm Eck and the Neues Kranzler Eck ('Eck' means corner) are glass and steel structures that have added new style and glamour to the Ku'damm. The latter is named after

Café Kranzler, Kurfürstendamm, Charlottenburg

Café Kranzler which moved here in the 1950s and occupied a large site on the corner of Joachimstaler Straße. Its much reduced version still has good views across the Ku'damm.

Tauentzienstraße

Tauentzienstraße seems busier than the Ku'damm because so many shops are concentrated along its comparatively short length and the pavements are not so wide. Among the central flower beds and benches a massive steel sculpture called 'Berlin' expresses the 'broken' nature of the city during the Cold War. Opposite Wittenbergplatz U-Bahn station is the largest department store on the continent, the prestigious 'KaDeWe', short for Kaufhaus des Westens (Department Store of the West). Both buildings have been faithfully reconstructed since the war.

Schloss Charlottenburg Charlottenburg Palace

This exquisite royal palace is about 15 minutes by bus (109) from Zoo Station. It was destroyed during the bombing and has been meticulously recreated from the original plans. Schloss Charlottenburg belonged to the House of

Charlottenburg Palace

Hohenzollern and was built between 1695 and 1699 as the summer residence for Sophie Charlotte, wife of Elector Friedrich III and a great patron of artists and philosophers. The cupola and orangery were added in 1701 when Friedrich became the first Prussian King. It was later transformed into a miniature Versailles by his grandson Frederick the Great who built a new wing in Rococo style. The theatre at the end of the orangery and the Belvedere teahouse in the grounds were designed by Langhans. In 1810 Friedrich Wilhelm III commissioned Schinkel to build a mausoleum for his deceased wife, Luise, and also the Neuer Pavillon as a summer retreat. Two stone warriors guard the entrance to the courtyard of the palace with its large equestrian statue of the Great Elector, Friedrich Wilhelm I, designed in 1698 by Andreas Schlüter. It originally stood in front of the Stadtschloss and was removed for safekeeping during the war. The barge which brought it back to Berlin sank to the bottom of the Tegeler See where it lay until salvaged in 1949.

Schloss Charlottenburg consists of the Altes Schloss (Old Palace) and the Neuer Flügel (New Wing) and further buildings in the Schlossgarten (park). Each section charges a separate admission, but entrance to the grounds is free. The elegance of the baroque decorations in the rooms of the Altes Schloss proves that there was more to the Prussian monarchy than military ambition. They are a dazzling spectacle of Gobelin tapestries,

French paintings and gilded stucco work. The Porzellankabinett has mirrored walls, a glorious painted ceiling and a fine collection of oriental porcelain. Next to it is the splendid Schlosskapelle (Palace Chapel). The Neuer Flügel includes the opulent State Apartments of Frederick the Great and the more modest Winter Chambers of Friedrich Wilhelm II, but the real highlights are the Goldene Galerie and the Weißer Saal (White Hall). The restored Neuer Pavillon contains a collection of paintings and sculptures.

On the western side of the palace is the Große Orangerie, used for exhibitions and concerts. Behind it an avenue of fir trees leads to the Mausoleum, a mock Doric temple where a number of Prussian rulers are buried, including Queen Luise, whose tomb features her famous reclining marble effigy designed by Christian Daniel Rauch. In the north-eastern corner of the Schlosspark on the banks of the Spree is the Belvedere, containing a fabulous porcelain museum. The palace grounds were originally laid out in the French Baroque style but later converted into an English landscaped park. After the war the area behind the palace was turned back into a formal French garden.

Olympiastadion

Berlin's Olympic Stadium is about 20 minutes by S-Bahn or U-Bahn from Zoo station. It was originally built for the 1936 Berlin Olympics in the southern part of the Reichssportfeld (now Olympiapark Berlin) and is a monumental complex with the Olympic square, the 'Maifeld' where huge rallies could be staged, a swimming stadium, a hockey stadium, several other huge buildings and a number of statues expressing the National Socialist obsession with the ideal body and state-approved values. Also unveiled in 1936 was the Waldbühne, a huge open-air arena in the style of an ancient Greek theatre. The area suffered little damage in the war and during Berlin's division the British had their headquarters in the northern part. The Olympiastadion is still used as an athletics stadium but has strong soccer traditions; it is the home ground of the Berlin football team, Hertha BSC and the German cup final is also held here every year. It underwent extensive renovation for the 2006 FIFA World Cup when it hosted six matches, including the final. 70% of the original structure was retained and the bombastic bulk of the 1930s Nazi stadium remains. The most striking changes are the blue track and the new roof whose transparent panels cover almost all the 75,000 seats. It makes a perfect venue for big music concerts as well as sporting events. On non-event days you can visit the stadium individually and use a multi-language audio-guide or join one of the excellent hour-long guided tours in English. (www.olympiastadion-berlin.de)

The 'Glockenturm' (Bell Tower) is a 145 metre observation tower built by the Nazis in 1934 to house the Olympic Bell. It provides great views for miles around as well as a bird's eye perspective of the whole grandiose Olympic complex. The tower was modernised for the 2006 World Cup and a new glass lift installed. At ground level there is an excellent exhibition about the 1936 Olympics and the history of the site.

Funkturm Radio Tower

There are also good views of West Berlin from the Funkturm (radio tower) opened in 1926 in the Messegelände (exhibition area). It resembles the Eiffel Tower and was originally planned as a transmitting tower. Later additions were a restaurant at 55 metres and an observation deck at 125 metres, both served by an express lift. The Funkturm is illuminated at night and Berliners call it "der lange Lulatsch" (the lanky lad). The nearest stations are Messe Nord or Kaiserdamm.

Tiergarten

Tiergarten ('animal garden') is the name of both the huge city centre park and its surrounding district. The park was designed in the 1830s by landscape architect Peter Joseph Lenné and was originally a hunting ground for the Kurfürsten (Electors of Brandenburg). The city's main east-west axis cuts through the centre of the Tiergarten and this stretch is called 'Straße des 17. Juni'(17th June Street) to recall the 1953 workers' uprising in East Berlin. The Siegessäule (victory column), erected in 1873 after the Prussians had won several wars, originally stood on the square in front of the Reichstag but Hitler had it moved to the 'Großer Stern' (large star) to form the centre-piece of his Siegesallee (victory avenue). The Berlin nickname for the column is 'Goldelse' (Golden Lizzy) and it is flanked by impressive statues of great Prussian statesmen and generals. It survived the bombing but the Tiergarten was a wasteland; all the trees had either been destroyed or used as firewood and after the war, when food was short, it was used for growing vegetables. Now the new trees have matured and this is a well-loved park. There is a pretty lake and waterways and some beautiful walks; one path leading from the Siegessäule has ceremonial sculptures of Prussian aristocrats enacting an 18th century hunt.

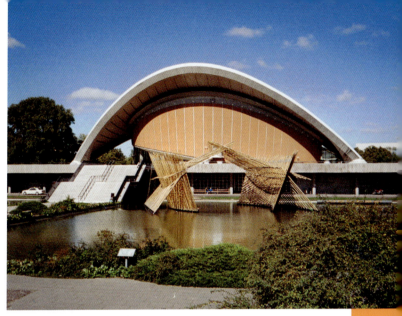

Haus der Kulturen der Welt, Tiergarten

There are two significant buildings on the northern edge of the Tiergarten. Schloss Bellevue is the official residence of the German President, a white palace set in immaculate gardens running down to the Spree. It was built in 1785 as a summer residence for the younger brother of Frederick the Great and members of the Hohenzollern family lived here until 1918. The Haus der Kulturen der Welt (House of World Cultures) with its strange-shaped roof was originally the Kongresshalle (Congress Hall), presented to Berlin in 1957 by the USA. Next to it is the Carillon, a tower with 68 bells which automatically play a tune at 12 noon and 6pm daily. There are also concerts on summer Sunday afternoons.

Central Berlin

The post-Wall central area of Berlin is mainly located in former West Berlin and contains the new government district, a collection of prestigious new government buildings lined up along the Spree and Potsdamer Platz, Berlin's mammoth new high-rise development. This glamorous vision of one of Berlin's most famous pre-war squares creates an impressive skyline as it bursts upwards into the Brandenburg sky and breathes life back into the death zone.

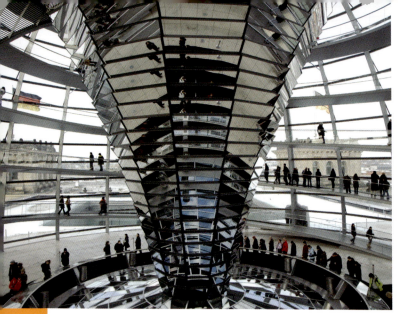

Inside the huge glass dome of the Reichstag

The Reichstag

The Reichstag is the most symbolic of parliament buildings; a beacon of democracy in a city which has been subjected to two dictatorships. The word 'Reichstag' means 'Imperial Parliament' and goes back the days of German Unification in 1871 when the first Reichstag was assembled under Bismarck. The Federal Parliament of today's Germany is the 'Bundestag' which has its seat in the 'Reichstagsgebäude' (the Imperial parliament building). It was constructed between 1884 and 1894, mainly funded with reparation money from the Franco-Prussian War of 1871 and the huge inscription 'Dem Deutschen Volke' (for the German People) was added in 1916 by Kaiser Wilhelm II using bronze letters cast from captured French cannons.

When Kaiser Wilhelm II abdicated in 1919 the German Republic was proclaimed from one of the balconies and the building continued to serve as the seat of parliament during the Weimar Republic. This ended on 30th January 1933 when Adolf Hitler was appointed Reichskanzler. The infamous Reichstag fire soon followed, allegedly started by an unemployed communist bricklayer from Holland and used by Hitler as a pretext to ban the Communist Party. He then gained the parliamentary majority he needed to pass the Enabling Act, giving the Nazi Party unlimited powers. During the Third Reich the Reichstag building was only used for propaganda presentations and by

Bundeskanzleramt, Tiergarten

the military, but in April 1945 it became the central target for the invading Red Army, despite having served no political purpose for 12 years. The famous photograph of Soviet soldiers flying the Red Flag from one of the towers was staged a few days after they had taken the building and visitors can still see the Russian graffiti on the walls. During the Berlin Blockade of 1948–49 a huge crowd of West Berliners assembled in front of the Reichstag to hear their Mayor, Ernst Reuter, make an impassioned plea to the 'peoples of the world'. After the West German capital moved to Bonn in 1949, the Reichstag was crudely rebuilt without its cupola and used for a rather dull exhibition on German history.

Its role changed dramatically after the Wall fell. The official reunification ceremony and celebrations were held at the Reichstag on 3rd October 1990 and the parliament of a united Germany symbolically assembled inside the building the next day. In 1991 a slim parliamentary majority decided to move the German capital back to Berlin, but before work started on the Reichstag building it was 'wrapped' by the famous artist Christo in 1995. The following year, Sir Norman Foster won the architectural contest for reconstructing the Reichstag. He reintroduced the idea of a glass cupola and his 21st century version has been a spectacular success. In 1999 the German Bundestag moved into the renovated Reichstag building, with its state of the art interior.

It is now the most visited parliament in the world. The views from inside the cupola are fantastic and the fact that visitors can 'look down on' the politicians in the main chamber sends a clear message about democracy. Entrance to the Reichstag dome is free, but you must book your visit in advance or reserve a table at the Käfer restaurant on the roof terrace. It is also well worth booking a guided tour in order to see inside the whole building.
| www.bundestag.de

Memorials

The space in front of the Reichstag is a grassed-over area where people fly kites or kick a football around. It is hard to imagine the battle scenes that must have raged here in the last days of the war, but on the other side of Scheidemannstraße there is an impressive Soviet war memorial set in landscaped gardens on the edge of the Tiergarten. It was built in October 1945, close to where thousands of Red Army soldiers lost their lives in the final Battle for Berlin and is also a cemetery for 2,500 of the casualties. Just a few metres from the south-west corner of the Reichstag building is a memorial consisting of 96 slate plates set into the cobblestones. Each slate plate represents one of the 96 Social Democrat and Communist Reichstag delegates who were murdered during the Third Reich. On the corner of Scheidemannstraße and Ebertstraße is a row of white crosses to commemorate East Germans who were shot trying to escape to West Berlin across the Spree and to the right of the Brandenburg Gate is the Memorial to the Murdered Jews of Europa (Holocaust Memorial) described in 'Jewish Berlin' (page 180).

Regierungsviertel Government District

The sleek corporate office park of Berlin's new government district was completed in 2003. The most eye-catching buildings are the Bundeskanzleramt (Federal Chancellery) and the Paul-Löbe-Haus and the Marie-Elisabeth-Lüders Haus, linked by a two tier glass and steel walkway across the river. On the other side of the Reichstag the Jakob-Kaiser-Haus on the Reichstagufer is the largest of all the parliamentary office buildings. Outside it stand 19 large glass posters featuring articles of the Grundgesetz (Basic German Law), a clever juxtaposition of transparency and democratic precepts. The central part of the Bundeskanzleramt is cube-shaped and has earned the nickname 'die Waschmaschine' (washing machine). The grand foyer can be seen through the glass wall and the Chancellor's office enjoys the finest

The Reichstag, Tiergarten

views of the modern capital. The new Hauptbahnhof shimmers in the background and beneath the ground the new U55 line shuttles visitors back and forth to Unter den Linden. The best way of seeing this area is to take a Spree river cruise. An hour's return trip from the Berliner Dom covers most of the new government buildings as well as the historic centre of East Berlin.

Potsdamer Platz

The other huge new development in the central area of Berlin has more to do with business and pleasure than politics. The original pre-war Potsdamer Platz was the equivalent of New York's Times Square or London's Piccadilly Circus until it was flattened by a combination of bombs, tanks and a death strip. Its resurrection was brought about by international investment and the most prestigious architects available. The foundation stone was laid in 1994 and for the 'topping-out' ceremony in 1996 Daniel Barenboim conducted construction cranes as they 'danced' to Beethoven's Ninth Symphony.

Potsdamer Platz has three distinct parts. The flashy Sony Center is built round a central plaza covered with a dramatic tent-like glass roof radiating different colours at night and is the perfect setting for 'cinema city' during

Potsdamer Platz, Mitte/Tiergarten

the Berlin Film Festival. It also features the original Kaisersaal (Imperial room) from the Hotel Esplanade whose neo-baroque façade has been preserved on Bellevuestraße. Daimler City, on the other side of Potsdamer Straße, stars Renzo Piano's stone-glass 22 floor Debis Tower, the Daimler Group's Headquarters and contains the historic 'Weinhaus Huth', the only building left standing during the years of division, the 'Potsdamer Arkaden' shopping mall and two modern theatres. On the northern edge is the brick-clad Kollhoff building and at the top of this 25 storey office block is the Panoramapunkt, with an open-air viewing platform and an excellent photographic exhibition of the history of Potsdamer Platz. The express lift takes 20 seconds to reach the top and the views are superb, both from the terraces and the stylish café-bar. The third slice of Potsdamer Platz, between the Sony Center and Ebertstraße, is the more classic Beisheim Center, inspired by elegant Manhattan skyscraper design and showcasing two five star hotels.

Kulturforum Cultural Forum

This area was developed when West Berlin had to create its own separate cultural life and was masterminded by one of the most important architects

The Italian Embassy, Tiergarten

of the 1950s, Hans Scharoun. The buildings are grouped randomly around St Matthäus-Kirche, a restored Italian byzantine-style church, designed by August Stüler in 1844–46. The church is the sole survivor of this pre-war high-society neighbourhood which Hitler had already started to clear in the 1930s as part of his plans for the 'World City Germania'. The Kulturforum includes the Philharmonie, home of the Berlin Philharmonic, the Kammermusiksaal (Chamber Music Hall), the Neue Nationalgalerie (New National Gallery), the Gemäldegalerie (Old Masters Gallery) the Kunstgewerbemuseum (Applied Arts Museum), the Musikinstrumentenmuseum (Musical Instrument Museum) and a branch of the Staatsbibliothek (State Library).

Next to the Kulturforum is the 'Diplomatenviertel' an embassy district which developed around Tiergartenstraße in the late 19th century, when a newly united Imperial Germany was growing in international importance. Most of these buildings were destroyed in the war but two Nazi era buildings survived – the Italian and Japanese embassies, stranded in a wasteland. What was once Mussolini's huge marble palace became a home to stray goats. It was extensively renovated in 2003 and new life has been breathed into this area. It is worth exploring the surrounding streets to appreciate the modern architecture of the new embassies.

City Centre Sights

Cool Collections

The story of Berlin's museums and galleries is unique. In the 18th and 19th centuries the culture-crazy Prussian elite established rich foundations and Imperial Berlin continued the process. A new era of collecting began during the Cold War. The fierce competitiveness between the two political systems meant that both halves of the city wanted to show off their prized possessions and communicate their own version of historical events. State subsidies financed new initiatives in West Berlin and Berlin's museums multiplied. Since reunification there has been a reshuffling of collections and some exciting new ventures.

But it's not just the exhibits that are interesting, it's the buildings themselves. Grand old structures have been imaginatively restored, tenement blocks, warehouses and bunkers have been cleverly adapted and there are striking contemporary pavilions.

The most high-profile project is the rebirth of the five temple-style museums on Museumsinsel (Island of Museums). During the city's division these collections were locked away in East Berlin and some of the buildings stood as ruins for decades. West Berlin's response in the 1960s was to create the Kulturforum, a complex of concert halls, museums and galleries designed by Hans Scharoun and built on the wasteland near Potsdamer Platz. There is also a cluster of art museums around Schloss Charlottenburg and several collections in Dahlem. The national collections are part of the Staatliche Museen zu Berlin (SMB) and are closed on Mondays, as are many of the others. Museums associated with Jewish Berlin, Hitler's Berlin, Divided Berlin and the Berlin Wall are described in the 'Special Dossier'.

English speakers have excellent access to all the Berlin collections and there are often free guided tours in English. They are relatively cheap to visit, especially if you make use of the three day Museumspass, combination tickets or reductions offered with the BVG travel cards. Museum fanatics should visit Berlin for one of the 'Lange Nacht der Museen' (the Long Night of Museums) at the end of January or the end of August. Details of opening times, entrance fees and the exact location of each museum can be found at: **www.museumsportal-berlin.de**.

Akademie der Künste

Berlin's Academy of Arts, founded in 1696, is its oldest and most prestigious cultural institution and has a fabulous location on Pariser Platz. There are excellent temporary exhibitions and the 'Weinwirtschaft' café is an insider tip for lunch.

| 4 Pariser Platz, 10117 Berlin-Mitte, www.adk.de

Alte Nationalgalerie (SMB)

The Alte Nationalgalerie on Museumsinsel contains Berlin's fine collection of paintings from the French Revolution to the First World War. Built between 1867 and 1876 it stands majestically like a Greek temple alongside the Spree, encapsulating Berlin's Prussian aspirations to become the new Athens of the North. By 1955 all its rooms were open to the public and now it has been fully restored. The 19th century grandeur of the interior has been preserved, complete with marble staircases and red carpets. Highlights are the jewels of German Romanticism, with paintings by Caspar David Friedrich and Carl Blechen, wonderful Berlin views by Eduard Gärtner, huge paintings by Adolph Menzel depicting subjects of Prussian history and a rich collection of Impressionist masterpieces. Among the 19th century sculptures are famous works by Schadow as well as some early Rodins.

| 1-3 Bodestraße, 10178 Berlin-Mitte, www.smb.museum/ang

Altes Museum (SMB)

The oldest museum on Museumsinsel was opened in 1829. Schinkel's neo-classical design radiates the cultural gravitas of ancient Greece and embodies Wilhelm von Humboldt's idea of the museum as a public educational institution. The monumental order of the 18 fluted ionic columns, the spacious atrium, the rotunda modelled on the Pantheon in Rome and the grand staircase are architectural elements previously reserver for stately buildings. It originally housed the Berlin art collections in their entirety, but since 1904 the Altes Museum has contained parts of the collection of Classical Antiquities.

It also stages high-profile temporary exhibitions. During the GDR years it stood grandly but forlornly, looking across a drab, grey square. Now both the museum and the Lustgarten have been returned to their original splendour. Humboldt and Schinkel would be very satisfied.

| Am Lustgarten, 10178 Berlin-Mitte, www.smb.museum/am

Alte Nationalgalerie, Museumsinsel, Mitte

Bauhaus-Archiv

This Museum and Institute of Design is devoted to the history and influence of the Bauhaus School of Architecture, Design and Art (1919–33). The building is a late work of Walter Gropius, founder of the Bauhaus movement, and its white silhouette is one of West Berlin's post-war landmarks. The entire spectrum of the Bauhaus School's activities is on display and there are often special exhibitions. The museum shop has a selection of Bauhaus-style merchandise and the café is worth a visit too. It has lovely views of the canal and of Villa von der Heydt, apparently used as an opium den by the Chinese Embassy in the 1880s and one of the last mansions in Tiergarten to survive Albert Speer's development plans for Hitler's new capital.

| 14 Klingelhöferstraße, 10785 Berlin-Tiergarten, www.bauhaus.de

Berliner Medizinhistorisches Museum

The Berlin Medical History Museum opened in 1899 with Rudolf Virchow's famous pathological-anatomical collection of specimens and is not for the squeamish. Located in the grounds of the Charité Hospital overlooking the Spree, this fascinating museum traces the development of medicine over the past 400 years, with particular emphasis on the work at the historic Charité

Cool Collections

which started as a Plague Hospital in 1710 and on Berlin's role in the world of medical research. The original Virchow lecture hall has been preserved as a wartime ruin and is used for seminars and private events.
| 1 Charitéplatz, 10117 Berlin-Mitte, www.bmm.charite.de

Berlinische Galerie

This collection of Modern Art, Photography and Architecture, one of Berlin's youngest and most experimental museums, is in a former glass warehouse which includes an 11 metre high hall. The permanent collection features works from 1870 to the present day. In summer the café spills out on to the lettered forecourt, with its huge steel sculpture.
| 124–128 Alte Jakobstraße, 10969 Berlin-Kreuzberg, www.berlinischegalerie.de

Bode-Museum (SMB)

The Baroque style Bode-Museum sits regally at the end of Museumsinsel like the prow of a stately galleon and appears to rise from the waters of the Spree. It was commissioned by Kaiser Wilhelm II as the 'Kaiser Friedrich-Museum' and opened in 1904 as a museum for European Renaissance art. In 1956 it was renamed after the influential General Director of Museums, Wilhelm von Bode. Its treasures now include impressive Byzantine works of art, a wonderful collection of sculptures from the Middle Ages to the 18th century and a fine coin collection. The beautifully-renovated halls devoted to the Italian Renaissance and the German late Gothic school are breathtaking.
| 1 Am Kupfergraben, 10178 Berlin-Mitte, www.smb.museum/bm

Brecht-Weigel-Gedenkstätte

125 Chausseestraße was the last home of poet and playwright Bertolt Brecht and his wife, actress Helene Weigel. Brecht returned to East Berlin after spending the war in the USA and created the acclaimed Berliner Ensemble theatre company. He lived here from October 1953 until his death in August 1956 and is buried in the pretty Dorotheenstadt cemetery next to the building. There are guided tours of the artists' living and working rooms and the Brecht-Weigel archives. The excellent 'Kellerrestaurant' (open in the evenings) is decorated with authentic family photographs and set props.
| 125 Chausseestraße, 10115 Berlin-Mitte,
www.adk.de/de/archiv/gedenkstaetten/gedenkstaetten-brecht-weigel.htm

Bode-Museum, Museumsinsel, Mitte

Bröhan-Museum

This treasure chest of art, crafts and furniture from the eras of Art Nouveau, Art Deco and Functionalism (1889–1939) is named after Karl Bröhan who donated his priceless collection to Berlin on his 60th birthday. The ground floor has room ensembles, the first floor is a picture gallery and the third floor houses special exhibitions. The fine building is part of a converted 'Garde du Corps' infantry barracks across the road from Schloss Charlottenburg.

| 1a Schloßstraße, 14059 Berlin-Charlottenburg, www.broehan-museum.de

Brücke-Museum

The revolutionary 'Brücke' movement was the creation of four architecture students in 1905 and critical to the development of Expressionism. Initially comprising a donation of 74 paintings in 1964, the Brücke-Museum now has over 400 paintings and sculptures as well as countless drawings. The flat-roofed, one-storey building among the tall birch and pine trees on the edge of the Grunewald follows the Bauhaus tradition and provides a perfect setting. Exhibitions focus on individual members of the Brücke. It is closed on Tuesdays.

| 9 Bussardsteig, 14195 Berlin-Dahlem, www.bruecke-museum.de

Buchstaben Museum

This unique Museum of Letters – the typographical kind – has a huge collection of fascinating 'characters'. Opening hours are generally Thursday, Friday and Saturday afternoons.

| 13 Karl-Liebknecht-Straße, 10178 Berlin-Mitte, www.buchstabenmuseum.de

Daimler Contemporary

A loft-like gallery in the historic Haus Huth building on Potsdamer Platz holds exhibitions of works from a collection over 1,800 started in 1977.

| 5 Alte Potsdamer Straße, 10785 Berlin-Tiergarten,
www.sammlung.daimler.com/contemporary/contemporary_e.htm

Dali-Museum

The Berlin Dali exhibition on Leipziger Platz is a comprehensive cross section of the artist's work with over 400 exhibits. Dali 'scouts' are on hand to guide visitors.

| 7 Leipziger Platz, 10117 Berlin-Mitte, www.daliberlin.de

Deutsches Currywurst Museum

The Currywurst epitomises the very essence of Berlin – a spiced-up version of something German. This place is great interactive fun for Currywurst fans.

| 70 Schützenstraße, 10117 Berlin-Mitte, www.currywurstmuseum.de

Deutsche Guggenheim Berlin

The sleek gallery on the ground floor of the historic Deutsche Bank building on Unter den Linden has several exhibitions a year showcasing works from the Guggenheim's extensive collection. The 'Kaffeebank' and the shop selling art books and gifts are both popular with Berliners.

| 13/15 Unter den Linden, 10117 Berlin-Mitte, www.deutsche-guggenheim.de

Deutsches Historisches Museum

The Museum of German History occupies the oldest building on Unter den Linden, the former 'Zeughaus' (Armoury). In 1939 all army museums were taken over by the Nazis who used the Zeughaus and its beautiful courtyard

Deutsches Historisches Museum, Mitte

to propagate their own version of German heroism. When it reopened in 1952 it then contained the GDR interpretation of German history from the Marxist-Leninist point of view. This collection was dissolved in 1990, the building was refurbished and the new exhibition opened in 2006. The huge model in the entrance hall gives an interesting overview of German territories through the ages and the three floors of the museum cover all aspects of German history from the 9th century to the present. The descriptive labels are well-designed and thorough and there are some good inter-active spots. The museum also has a stunning modern extension, the I. M. Pei building, used for its superb temporary exhibitions. The splendid Café im Zeughaus faces the Kupfergraben.

| 2 Unter den Linden, 10117 Berlin-Mitte, www.dhm.de

Deutsche Kinemathek – Museum für Film und Fernsehen

This museum in the Sony Center charts the fascinating legacy of German film history, from the pioneering days and silent films, the culture boom of the Weimar Republic, the propaganda films during the Nazi period, the exodus to Hollywood after 1933, to post-war films and digital films. Special sections are

devoted to Marlene Dietrich and the careers of German film directors who made history with their films. The exhibition on television covers seven decades of German TV and there is plenty to enjoy in the Filmhaus shop and bistro.
| 2 Potsdamer Straße, 10785 Berlin-Tiergarten, www.deutsche-kinemathek.de

Deutsch-Russisches Museum

It was here, in the Officers' Mess of a former Wehrmacht engineers' school, that the German armed forces signed the unconditional surrender to the Soviets on 8th May 1945. From 1967 the building was used as a Soviet museum about the Battle for Berlin and the capitulation. In 1990 the Russians and Germans agreed on a joint venture and the permanent exhibition now focuses on German-Soviet relations between 1917 and 1990. Sadly, the wonderful model of the Battle for Berlin from the GDR years has apparently been taken back to Moscow but the Russians left behind the display of armoured vehicles in the gardens, a rather bizarre sight in 21st century suburban Berlin. Café Paulines near Karlshorst station is recommended for local atmosphere.
| 4 Zwieseler Straße, 10318 Berlin-Karlshorst, www.museum-karlshorst.de

Deutsches Technikmuseum

Berlin's impressive scientific and technical collections go back over 120 years. The extension for the aviation and maritime collections is a prominent city landmark as one of the aircraft used in the Berlin Airlift is suspended dramatically from its façade. The museum occupies a historic site, the former goods yard of Anhalter Station, dating back to 1874. It is popular with younger visitors and after 3pm entrance is free for under-18 year olds.

The Sugar Museum, Zeiss Planetarium and the Archenhold Observatory also belong to the Deutsches Technikmuseum but are in other parts of Berlin.
| 9 Trebbiner Straße, 10963 Berlin-Kreuzberg, www.sdtb.de

Ephraim-Palais

This fabulous building is an accurate reconstruction of a Rococo palace built in 1762 for the Jewish court jeweller, Veitel Heine Ephraim, and mounts first-class temporary exhibitions on Berlin's art and cultural history. Admission is free on the first Wednesday of each month.
| 16 Poststraße, 10178 Berlin-Mitte, www.stadtmuseum.de

Ephraim-Palais, Mitte

Ethnologisches Museum (SMB)

A gigantic archive of the world's cultural diversity, the Museum of Ethnology is currently part of the museum complex in West Berlin's Dahlem district. Founded in 1873, it houses half a million pre-industrial objects, acquired from the German voyages of exploration and German colonies.
| 27 Arnimallee, 14195 Berlin-Dahlem, www.smb.museum/em

Friedrichswerdersche Kirche (SMB)

The red brick neo-Gothic Schinkel church behind St Hedwigs-Kathedrale was named after Friedrich Wilhelm 'The Great Elector' and built between 1824 and 1830. The high vaulted ceiling of the nave makes a stunning setting for the early 19th century sculptures, part of the Nationalgalerie's collection. In the gallery is the 'Schinkel-Museum'. Admission is free.
| Werderscher Markt, 10117 Berlin-Mitte, www.smb.museum/fwk

Gemäldegalerie (SMB)

One of Berlin's best kept secrets, the 'Old Masters Gallery' is a fabulous collection of classical European paintings created in 1830 from the treasures

belonging to Prussian royalty. During the Cold War the collection was divided between East and West Berlin and the two halves have been reunited in a wonderfully light and spacious modern building in the Kulturforum. The main galleries are cleverly arranged in a horseshoe around a long central space described as a 'meditation hall'. There are 72 rooms with over 1,500 masterpieces including famous works by Botticelli, Bruegel, Caravaggio, Cranach, Dürer, Gainsborough, Raphael, Rembrandt, Rubens, Vermeer, Watteau – the list is endless. There is an excellent shop and restaurant too.
| Matthäikirchplatz, 10785 Berlin-Tiergarten, www.smb.museum/gg

Georg-Kolbe-Museum

Georg Kolbe (1877–1947) was one of the most prolific German sculptors of the first half of the 20th century. A great exponent of the idealistic nude, his style was a definite departure different from traditional monumental sculpture. This collection in his studio home in Charlottenburg is a summary of his work in sculpture and drawing. 'Café K' has an enchanting garden setting, perfect for summer brunch or afternoon tea.
| 25 Sensburger Allee, 14055 Berlin-Charlottenburg,
www.georg-kolbe-museum.de

Hamburger Bahnhof, Museum für Gegenwart (SMB)

Berlin's Museum of Contemporary Art is in a converted railway station. The grand industrial hall and the inner courtyard have been retained and at night the station's impressive neo-classical façade is bathed in blue and green neon light. The exhibition area with its glass roofs and geometric designs is dedicated to art from the second half of the 20th century onwards and includes the Marx collection of drawings by Beuys and Warhol. The 'Rieckhallen' built on the site of the former 'Lehrter' station contain the controversial Flick Collection. The Sarah Wiener restaurant has a good reputation among Berliners.
| 50–51 Invalidenstraße, 10557 Berlin-Tiergarten, www.hamburgerbahnhof.de

Hanfmuseum

This museum in the Nikolaiviertel is devoted to the many uses of cannabis. There is a Lesecafé (Reading Café) which doubles as an artists' gallery.
| 5 Mühlendamm, 10178 Berlin-Mitte, www.hanfmuseum.de

Deutsches Technikmuseum, Kreuzberg

Haus am Waldsee

The Haus am Waldsee was built as a private mansion on the edge of the Grunewald in 1922. After the war it became a refugee camp for the arts and while Berlin was still in ruins the Berlin Philharmonic Orchestra played its first post-war concert here in 1945.

Today it is an important exhibition space for international contemporary artists, designers, musicians and writers. The beautiful gardens behind the house have sculptures dotted among the trees and on the lawns that lead down to the lake. One exhibit is the 'Loftcube', which can be lowered by helicopter on to the rooftops of tall buildings, ideal for urban nomads in high-rise cities.

In summer the café serves coffee and cake on the terrace.

| 30 Argentinische Allee, 14163 Berlin-Zehlendorf, www.hausamwaldsee.de

Käthe-Kollwitz-Musem

Käthe Kollwitz (1867–1945) is most famous for the 'Pieta' (mother with dead son) replicated in the Neue Wache and many of her sculptures and drawings embrace the more tragic aspects of life. In 1986 this wonderful exhibition of her works was opened in an elegant Charlottenburg mansion, although

Käthe Kollwitz lived and worked in Prenzlauer Berg, then a working-class neighbourhood. The museum's peaceful garden has a path leading to the Literaturhaus café next door.

| 24 Fasanenstraße, 10719 Berlin-Charlottenburg, www.kaethe-kollwitz.de/museum-en.htm

Knoblauchhaus

The oldest house in the Nikolaiviertel was commissioned by master craftsman Johann Christian Knoblauch in 1761 and stayed in the family until 1929. The rooms have the furniture and décor of the Biedermeier period (1815–48) giving a good idea of how the well-to-do lived, dressed and made their money. The family wine cellar has been turned into a traditional inn.

| 23 Poststraße, 10178 Berlin-Mitte, www.stadtmuseum.de/index3.php?museum=kh

KW Institute for Contemporary Art

A must-see for modern art enthusiasts, KW has no collection of its own but views itself as "a laboratory for communicating and advancing contemporary cultural developments". Founded in the early 1990s in an old margarine factory on trendy Auguststraße in Mitte, the KW buildings have five floors of exhibition space and six studios for resident artists. They surround a courtyard featuring the Café Bravo in a glass cube.

| 69 Auguststraße, 10117 Berlin-Mitte, www.kw-berlin.de

Kreuzberg Museum

This local museum tells the story of Berlin's diverse district of Kreuzberg. The first floor charts the housing and social development in the area and the second floor has an interesting exhibition on its 300 year history of immigration.

| 95a Adalbertstraße, 10999 Berlin-Kreuzberg, www.kreuzbergmuseum.de

Kunstgewerbe Museum (SMB)

Fans of fine craftsmanship will appreciate this collection of decorative arts from the Middle Ages to the present, all wonderfully displayed in a purpose-built pavilion in the Kulturforum. The cost of entrance is included with a ticket for the Gemäldegalerie next door.

| Matthäikirchplatz, 10785 Berlin-Tiergarten, www.smb.museum/kgm

Liebermann-Villa, Wannsee

Kupferstichkabinett (SMB)

The Kupferstichkabinett is in the same building as the Gemäldegalerie and is one of the four most important collections of graphic art in the world. Visitors can ask to view and study the art works of their choice from thousands of drawings, watercolours, pastels and oil sketches.

| Matthäikirchplatz, 10785 Berlin-Tiergarten, www.smb.museum/kk

Liebermann-Villa

Impressionist painter Max Liebermann spent his summers in a beautiful mansion by Lake Wannsee from 1910 until it was confiscated by the Nazis. The Jewish artist completed more than 200 paintings here, featured in the permanent exhibition. There are excellent temporary exhibitions too and visitors can enjoy the gardens and the delights of Café Max. The Villa is closed on Tuesdays.

| 3 Colomierstraße, 14109 Berlin-Wannsee, www.max-liebermann.de

me Collectors Room Berlin

The 'me' stands for 'moving energies' and this innovative gallery on Auguststraße presents the Olbricht Collection through a series of rotating exhibitions.

Thomas Olbricht gave up his medical practice to go into the family hair-care business, Wella, and became chairman of the board. His private collection now comprises over 3,000 works by about 250 artists. Paintings, sculptures, photographs and installations are displayed over two floors in a light and large exhibition space.

The café and lounge area are perfect places to exchange views.

| 68 Auguststraße, 10117 Berlin-Mitte, www.me-berlin.com

Museum Berggruen (SMB)

The splendid Stüler building next to the Bröhan Museum, opposite Schloss Charlottenburg, contains the extensive private collection of Heinz Berggruen. The core exhibition dedicates three floors to Picasso's paintings, sculptures and drawings. There are also 60 of Paul Klee's works, over 20 by Henri Matisse and sculptures by Alberto Giacometti.

| 1 Schloßstraße, 14059 Berlin-Charlottenburg, www.smb.museum/mb

Museum für Asiatische Kunst (SMB)

Part of the Dahlem museum complex, this is a significant collection of art from the Indo-Asian area from the 4th century BC to the present. Unfortunately for Berlin, many exhibits were taken to the Soviet Union after the war and were never returned.

| 40 Takustraße, 14195 Berlin-Dahlem, www.smb.museum/mak

Museum für Kommunikation

An imposing example of Wilhelmine neo-Baroque architecture complete with funky blue neon lighting, this building housed the world's first postal museum. Visitors are greeted by three friendly robots circling the atrium and invited to explore the past, present and future of communication.

| 16 Leipziger Straße, 10117 Berlin-Mitte, www.mfk-berlin.de

Museum für Naturkunde

Berlin's Natural History Museum is very large, very old and much-loved – as are some of its exhibits. The skeleton of a Brachiosaurus from Tendaguru in Africa is world-famous; it is over 22 metres long and 9 metres high. There are also 4.6 billion-year-old meteorites and over 1,000 minerals. The

Altes Museum, Museumsinsel, Mitte

Department of Zoology boasts an extinct quagga, a Tasmanian tiger and 'Bobby' the gorilla, a pre-war Berlin Zoo celebrity.

The museum was founded with the Berlin University in 1810 and Kaiser Wilhelm II opened the current building in 1889. It was reorganised and renovated after reunification and the hands-on 'Humboldt-Exploratorium' was opened for younger visitors.

| 43 Invalidenstraße, 10115 Berlin-Mitte, www.naturkundemuseum-berlin.de

Museum für Fotografie (SMB)

This cool collection just behind Zoo station is a former Prussian Officers Mess with a grand staircase and wonderfully proportioned rooms. Two floors are owned by the Helmut Newton Foundation and largeformat photos of the first naked women Newton took pictures of make a bold statement in the entrance area. Helmut Newton was born in Berlin in 1920, left for Australia in 1938 and revolutionised the world of photography with his erotic style. He donated 1,000 of his pictures to the Helmut Newton Foundation and his widow presented the collection as a gift to the city of Berlin. On the second floor in the Kaisersaal (Imperial Hall) is the Art Library's Photographic Collection.

| 2 Jebensstraße, 10623 Berlin-Charlottenburg, www.smb.museum/mf

Madame Tussauds

Only a few weeks after opening, the Berlin waxwork museum hit the headlines when a 41-year old German decapitated a wax figure of Adolf Hitler in order to win a bet. All the usual international suspects are here, as well as famous Germans.

| 74 Unter den Linden, 10117 Berlin-Mitte, www.madametussauds.com/berlin

Märkisches Museum

The name refers to the 'Mark' (principality) of Brandenburg which surrounds Berlin and this museum relates Berlin's history through a series of themed rooms. The distinctive red brick building dates from 1899–1908 and features a restored Gothic chapel and guildhall. One of the most fascinating exhibits is the 'Kaiserpanorama', a stereoscope with 19th century images. In front of the museum are seven original graffiti-covered segments of the Berlin Wall and behind it the Köllnischer Park has a bear pit, home to Berlin's two official city bears. On Märkisches Ufer by the Spree is the 'Historischer Hafen' (Historic Harbour) a collection of over 20 boats, covering 250 years of inland shipping. One of them has a café in summer.

| 5 Am Köllnischen Park, 10178 Berlin-Mitte,
www.stadtmuseum.de/index3.php?museum=mm

Martin-Gropius-Bau

Originally built as the Museum of Applied Arts in 1881, the Martin Gropius building is named after one of its architects, great-uncle of Bauhaus founder, Walter Gropius. It was designed in the style of the Italian Renaissance with a grand central atrium. Shimmering mosaics elegantly decorate the spaces between the windows on the exterior. The Berlin Wall once blocked out the light but now the Martin-Gropius-Bau grandly faces the Abgeordnetenhaus (Berlin House of Representatives, formerly the Prussian parliament building) and is a venue for high-profile exhibitions that attract huge crowds.

| 7 Niederkirchnerstraße, 10963 Berlin-Kreuzberg, www.gropiusbau.de

Musikinstrumenten-Museum

Aptly located behind the Philharmonie in the Kulturforum this museum has an impressive collection of musical instruments dating back to the 16th

Martin-Gropius-Bau, Kreuzberg

century. Historic highlights include Frederick the Great's flutes and Benjamin Franklin's glass harmonica. On Saturdays 'The Mighty Würlitzer', the largest cinema organ in Europe, strikes up at noon and on Sunday mornings there are recitals featuring historic instruments. An excellent audio guide is included in the price of admission, there are unusual CDs on sale and the SIM café serves hot meals.

| 1 Tiergartenstraße, 10785 Berlin-Tiergarten, www.sim.spk-berlin.de/mim_3.html

Neue Nationalgalerie (SMB)

The 'temple of light and glass', on the edge of the Kulturforum is a striking contemporary building designed by Mies van der Rohe and home of Berlin's great collection of 20th century European paintings and sculptures from classical modernism to the 1960s. The lower level contains the museum's permanent collection which includes famous works by Picasso, Munch, Klee, Kirchner, Dix and Kandinsky.

| 50 Potsdamer Straße, 10785 Berlin-Tiergarten, www.smb.museum/nng

Neues Museum (SMB)

Although the other museums on Museumsinsel were gradually rebuilt after the war, the Neues Museum remained untouched and became a ghostly overgrown ruin. In 2009 it emerged from its historic slumber and its restoration by the British architect, David Chipperfield, captured everyone's imagination. The original architect, Friedrich August Stüler was assigned in 1843 to build a 'new' museum for Berlin's collection of Egyptian art and other antiquities. He designed magnificent Egyptian rooms, a fake Greek temple and Pompeiian villa and the grand structure was filled with the loot from Prussia's busy archaeologists. Chipperfield didn't opt for a faithful copy of Stüler's design, but incorporated war damage and decay into his work. Grand white modern stairways sweep past old brick walls full of bullet marks, original columns still have fire damage, and there are only the remnants of original mosaics and murals on the ceilings and walls. The result is spectacular and the star attraction, the iconic bust of the Egyptian queen Nefertiti, has been elevated to diva status.

| 1 Bodestraße, 10178 Berlin-Mitte, www.neues-museum.de

Nolde Stiftung

Emil Nolde, a renowned Expressionist painter, liked to spend his winters in Berlin and this intimate gallery off the Gendarmenmarkt exhibits some of his colourful works.

| 55 Jägerstraße, 10117 Berlin-Mitte, www.nolde-stiftung.de

Pergamonmuseum (SMB)

Berlin's monumental trove of ancient treasures sits majestically astride Museumsinsel and contains three amazing collections: the Collection of Classical Antiquities, the Museum of the Near East, and the Museum of Islamic Art. The massive three-winged building was designed by Alfred Messel and constructed between 1910 and 1930.

The Pergamon Altar, the Market Gate of Miletus, the Ishtar Gate of Babylon and the façade of a Jordanian desert castle, all reconstructions of massive ancient edifices, are simply awesome, even if the legitimacy of their acquisition may be controversial. During the war they were walled in for protection.

| 5 Am Kupfergraben, 10117 Berlin-Mitte, www.smb.museum/pm

Neues Museum, Museumsinsel, Mitte

Ramones Museum

This shrine to the American rockband, Ramones, proves that the subculture of rebellion and punk rock from the days of the GDR is still alive and well.

| 23 Krausnickstraße, 10115 Berlin-Mitte, www.ramonesmuseum.com

Sammlung Boros

When the Boros Collection opened to the public, the unique location and spectacular installation of the works turned it into one of the major modern art attractions of the German capital. This huge Nazi-era bunker has a colourful history. Built in 1942 as an air-raid shelter, it survived the war, was used to store imported fruit for East Berliners, who called it the 'Banana Bunker' and then had a brief stint as a hardcore techno club. In 2003 Christian Boros acquired the bunker for his eclectic art collection and created a penthouse flat on the top floor.

Tickets to join one of the excellent guided tours need to be booked well in advance.

| 20 Reinhardtstraße, 10117 Berlin-Mitte, www.sammlung-boros.de

Sammlung Hoffmann

Each Saturday there are guided tours of the Hoffmanns' unique collection of contemporary art in a converted factory building. Reservation essential.
| 21 Sophienstraße, 10178 Berlin-Mitte, www.sammlung-hoffmann.de

Sammlung Scharf-Gerstenberg (SMB)

Surrealism, symbolism and industrial terror all feature strongly in this art collection started in 1910 by Otto Gerstenberg. There are now over 250 works of art, many by famous names such as Dali, Ernst, Goya, Klee, Manet, Picasso and Piranesi. They are displayed in the dramatic surroundings of the converted coach-house and Marstall (stables) of Schloss Charlottenburg which housed the Egyptian museum before it moved to the Neues Museum. The surrealism of Nefertiti's one-eyed beauty still haunts the lofty Marstall. The café has massive windows and good cake.
| 70 Schloßstraße, 14059 Berlin-Charlottenburg, www.smb.museum/ssg

Schwules Museum

Founded in 1985 above a gay nightclub, this was the world's first museum dedicated to homosexual topics. The permanent exhibition documents 200 Years of Gay History and temporary exhibitions often focus on gay icons.
| 61 Mehringdamm, 10961 Berlin-Kreuzberg, www.schwulesmuseum.de

The Kennedys

JFK captured the hearts of the Berliners when he made his historic visit in 1963. There are some fascinating Kennedy memorabilia on display here, including letters and film footage. The exhibition also underlines the compelling power of photography in promoting the Kennedys as iconic figures.
| 4a Pariser Platz, 10117 Berlin-Mitte, www.thekennedys.de

The Story of Berlin

This lively multi-media museum in the Ku'damm Karree off the Kurfürstendamm is a room by room account of Berlin's 800 years of history and includes a tour of the vast nuclear bomb shelter which runs underneath the building.
| 207–208 Kurfürstendamm, 10719 Berlin-Charlottenburg, www.story-of-berlin.de

The Story of Berlin nuclear bunker, Charlottenburg

"Wege, Irrwege, Umwege"
Museum of Parliamentary Democracy

The converted Deutscher Dom on Gendarmenmarkt with its spiral stone staircases makes a perfect setting for an exhibition documenting the 'Paths, wrong turnings, detours' of Germany's difficult journey to parliamentary democracy. Admission is free and English speakers are advised to hire an audio-guide.

| 1 Gendarmenmarkt, 10117 Berlin-Mitte,
www.bundestag.de/kulturundgeschichte/ausstellungen/wege

Zille Museum

A charming museum in the Nikolaiviertel is devoted to Heinrich Zille (1859–1929) whose famous sketches and photographs captured working-class life in Berlin with such humour and empathy.

| 11 Propststraße, 10178 Berlin-Mitte, www.heinrich-zille-museum.de

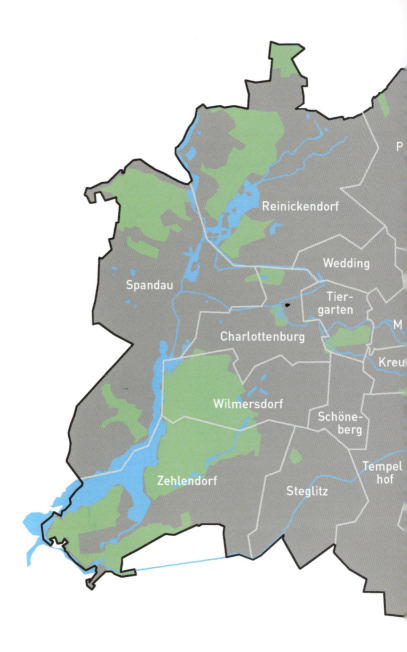

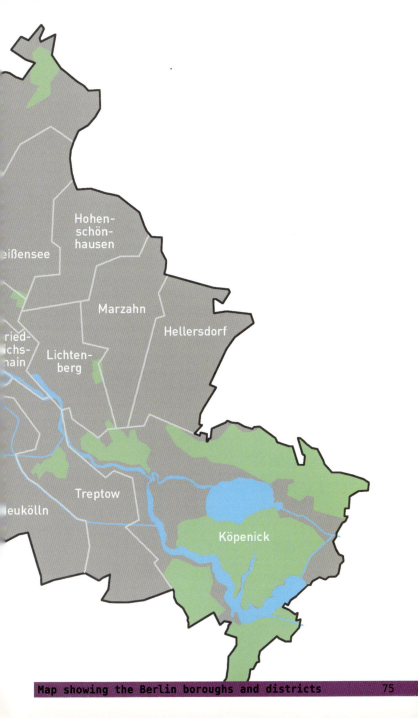

Map showing the Berlin boroughs and districts

Small Worlds

Despite the grandiose efforts of the Kaisers, the Nazis and the Communists, Berlin still has no absolute centre. It remains more or less an assembly of districts which were once towns or villages and within them are small worlds, often referred to by Berliners as their 'Kiez'. This word originally referred to a Slav fishing settlement, but gradually came to mean a working-class neighbourhood in Berlin. Now the term is applied to any urban district where there is a strong social network. Life revolves around the local shops and bars and the rest of Berlin is put at arm's length. This mentality is part of Berlin's great attraction as a place to live and one of the main reasons why so many people down the centuries have come to the city and ended up staying there. You can find your own niche and just hang out. That is the art of becoming a Berliner.

In 1920, when Greater Berlin was formed, it was organised into twenty 'Bezirke' (boroughs), each traditionally associated with a particular social class or political leaning. After the war, eight boroughs landed up in East Berlin and twelve in West Berlin. East Berlin later created three new ones when they constructed huge housing estates on the outskirts of the city. The years of division had political and social consequences, but most Berliners just got on with their lives and kept to their Kiez. The fall of the Wall caused a bigger shift in dynamics. Homes, businesses and shops sprouted up all over the place and there was a surge of immigrants especially from West Germany, Russia and Poland, as well as asylum seekers from the rest of the world. Cheap rents and new opportunities also attracted young Americans and West Europeans. In 2001, the 23 boroughs were officially amalgamated into twelve, but Berliners still think in terms of the old boroughs and the neighbourhoods within them.

This guide to Berlin's 'small worlds' includes tips on where to go and what to see. There are further restaurants and shops listed in 'Café Society' and 'Buy, Buy Berlin' and inside information on clubs is in 'Late Nightlife'. The 'Special Dossier' contains specific details of sites relating to Jewish, Nazi and GDR history and the Berlin Wall.

Mitte

Take me to Mitte, bitte! This is the borough in the middle of Berlin with a vibrant street life as well the main city centre sights. When the Berlin Wall came down, the neglected and run-down areas of 'Scheunenviertel' and 'Spandauer Vorstadt' were at the vanguard of the city centre's revival. These districts now have a largely young and fashionable population. They are in the thick of all the action, but have retained authentic charm.

Cafés and bars litter the square outside Hackescher Markt S-Bahn station and across the street **Weihenstephaner** serves Bavarian food and beer. In the historic Hackesche Höfe there are many more restaurants, although they tend to be full of tourists, rather than locals. The **Restaurant Hackescher Hof** and the **Oxymoron** are reliable choices. Almost next door to the Hackesche Höfe is Haus Schwarzenberg and **Café Cinema** by the entrance catches the Berlin feeling. In the courtyards are museums related to the Holocaust, fringe galleries, cafés and an arthouse cinema showing films in English. On Sophienstraße **Sophien 11** has old world charm and at **Mittendrin** you can lunch with the locals. There is also a lively scene at **Café Barcomi's** in the Sophie-Gips-Höfe, the interesting courtyards leading to Gipsstraße. At the end of Sophienstraße **Sophieneck** serves traditional Berlin fare.

There's a lot going on around Auguststraße too, with trendy but warm-hearted cafés and bars full of young and not so young locals. **Strandbad Mitte** and **Altes Europa** define the character of this neighbourhood. The temporary exhibitions at **Kunst-Werke** always provide a talking point. People spill out into the **Café Bravo**, an art exhibit in itself. Almost next door is the **me Collectors Room,** the latest in gallery experiences. There are several good restaurants, such as **Ruz** and **Restaurant Simon,** but a favourite haunt for all ages is **Clärchens Ballhaus** where time has stood still. Entire generations of lonely hearts have tried their luck here and it's still the best spot for upbeat ballroom dancing to live bands. Don't miss the amazing Spiegelsaal (mirrored room) on the first floor for pre-war atmosphere.

On the corner of Tucholskystraße a regular crowd gathers at the **Kayser Soze**, where the bar is open all hours and small cafés like **Buchhandlung** take off later in the evening. Just off Auguststraße, hidden away in the Heckmannhöfe is **Café Neu.** The setting is magical – three cobbled courtyards, a pretty fountain and small shops, including **Bonbonmacherei**, a traditional sweet factory. The courtyards lead through to Oranienburger Straße. There are several cafés on either side of the Neue Synagoge, but to really appreciate the warm spirit of this ancient Jewish neighbourhood, take a short walk round to **Beth Café** in Tucholskystraße.

Sophie-Gips-Höfe, Mitte

In Krausnickstraße is the whacky **Café Mania** in the **Ramones Museum**. Some of the apartment blocks here still follow the tradition of having a shop or business below street level, such as vegetarian café **Anna Koschke**. The next street is Große Hamburger Straße with several Jewish memorials. The aptly named café **You're Welcome** is a good place to restore the soul. The blackened and war-torn buildings masking St Sophienkirche contain **Kerzenkeller** selling all sorts of candles, **Viel Spiel,** a traditional toy shop, and **REmake,** perfect for a special lunch or dinner. Further along, opposite the grand old St Hedwigs Hospital, is **Schoko Galerie**, a treat for chocolate lovers. From Oranienburger Straße it is only a few minutes' walk down to Schiffbauerdamm with its row of lively restaurants and bars by the river Spree. **Ganymed**, **Brecht** and **Die Ständige Vertretung** all boast waterside terraces and each has a fascinating history and individual style. To escape the tourists, try the **Böse Buben Bar** on Marienstraße, where late risers go for all day breakfast.

There is much more to explore north of Auguststraße. Continue up Tucholskystraße past **Beth Café** and on the corner of Linienstraße **Bötzow-Privat** and **Schwarzwälderstuben** both have atmosphere. Walking along Linienstraße towards Koppenplatz when the street lamps are lit you can almost imagine the scene before Europe was thrown into two world wars.

Small Worlds

Brecht's Kellerrestaurant, Mitte

But the 21st century has turned this Kiez upside down. Turn left into Ackerstraße to find **Pro Macchina da Caffe** where the baristas serve one of the best espressos in Mitte. Further up Ackerstraße is **Markthalle VI,** one of the original Berlin market halls, beautifully restored on the outside but with its soul ripped out and replaced by modern shops. Don't dismiss Torstraße – this rather unpromising-looking main street is full of surprises. Scores of designer shops and the fashionable **Bandol sur Mer** restaurant rub shoulders with favourites such as **Tucholsky Restauration** and the **Kinderkaufhaus** toyshop, both reminiscent of GDR days. But the accent in Torstraße is now more 'socialite' than socialist. Its latest addition at the very eastern end is 'Soho House' a boutique hotel and exclusive members' club. This large Bauhaus building seems to echo the zeitgeist; it started life as a Jewish department store, became the Hitler Youth headquarters and then until 1989 housed the Communist Party archives before the Wall fell.

Rosenthaler Platz has some cheap eateries and the area around Weinbergspark is especially lively in summer. **Nola's am Weinberg,** once a faded GDR pavilion has been transformed by Swiss panache but the **Schwarze Pumpe** still has local colour. The buildings on Veteranenstraße used to form a gallery of squats, and anarchy reigns in the **Weinerei** where customers choose how much to pay for a glass of wine. Mitte extends up

Weinbergsweg as far as Zionskirchplatz. The Zionskirche has services in English on Sunday evenings and its vaulted ceilings provide an ethereal atmosphere for fashion shows. The tower is open on Sundays in summer. It has good views of this Kiez and the locals gather at **Roberta Bar** seven days a week. Just around the corner is Arkonaplatz, a large square with old Berlin charm, a flea market on Sundays and two good corner café-bars, **Alt-Berliner Kaffeestuben** and **Weltempfänger.**

At the western end of Torstraße is Chausseestraße. Try **La Bonne Franquette** for high ceilings, shabby chic and delicious French bistro food. The **Reinstoff** restaurant on Schlegelstraße is one of Berlin's newest stars in the Michelin galaxy. It has an old factory courtyard setting in the Edison Höfe, where Germany's first light bulbs were made and is not far from one of Berlin's best Jazz clubs, **Kunstfabrik Schlot**. Further down Chausseestraße is the **Kellerrestaurant** in the basement of Brecht's former home.

Mitte also includes Alexanderplatz and as city squares go they don't come much uglier. The smell of Bratwurst from the street-sellers lingers in the air around Alexanderplatz station, which hums with activity late into the night. The whole area is awash with high-rise GDR style office and apartment blocks. There is some warm Berlin hospitality on offer in the historic looking taverns of the Nikolaiviertel but this reconstruction of Berlin's medieval quarter is for tourists, not locals. The only genuine article in the vicinity is **Zur letzten Instanz.**

Wedding, Gesundbrunnen and Moabit

Although these districts are now part of Mitte they didn't experience the boom and gentrification of the 1990s. This is where you can still find the Berlin 'Schnauze mit Herz' (big mouth and big heart) of the working class and a social scene without pretension. In Wedding, a former borough of West Berlin and a communist stronghold in the 1920s, the residents are a rainbow assortment. **Schraders** in Malplaquetstraße is the extended living room for some of the locals and beer fans head for **Eschenbräu**. Gesundbrunnen is a gritty neighbourhood with the highest percentage of non-German residents of any Berlin locality. **Berliner Unterwelten** at Gesundbrunnen S-Bahn station offers fascinating tours of the world under Berlin's streets, including air-raid shelters and escape tunnels. In summer you can climb the surviving flak tower in the Humboldthain. For a taste of Kiez life try the **Bierbrunn** pub or a Currywurst from the Currybaude outside the station.

Gesundbrunnen Center, Wedding

Berliners associate Moabit, formerly part of the borough of Tiergarten, with prisons. The Kriminalgericht (main criminal court) is in Moabit and Berlin's largest detention centre is located nearby. A first prison, modelled on Pentonville Prison in London, was built in 1842 on Lehrter Straße and saw some illustrious inmates. It finally closed in 1955 and was later demolished. Its walls now enclose a small remembrance park, just north of the Hauptbahnhof. There are some interesting local haunts in Moabit. Just outside Birkenstraße U-Bahn station in the Stephanskiez neighbourhood is the **Dicker Engel**, a popular pub with a long Berlin history where the fat angel still hangs hopefully from the ceiling. **Arema** is also a good choice for local atmosphere. The **Arminius Markthalle** near Turmstraße U-Bahn is the most authentic of Berlin's three remaining market halls where the vaulted ceilings, small-paned windows and intricate carvings date back to 1891.

Tiergarten

The district of Tiergarten is now a part of Mitte. The city park itself has a regular clientele of local joggers, cyclists and dogwalkers and in summer the grassy areas are dotted with families enjoying a picnic. Berliners flock to the waterside at the **Café am See** or the **Schleusenkrug** and the restau-

Café Einstein, Tiergarten

rant ship **Capt'n Schillow** on the banks of the Spree. The **Tiergartenquelle** pub under the arches of Tiergarten station is a good place to meet the locals all year round. On the very eastern edge of Tiergarten is the original **Café Einstein** with vintage Viennese coffee house charm. Nearby Potsdamer Straße has the friendly **Joseph Roth Diele**, a traditional Berlin book café and after dark the chic 21st century **Victoria Bar.** This area is fast becoming the next big art location with galleries on upper floors or hidden in coutyards. The Freies Museum Berlin is a good place to start.

Prenzlauer Berg

Prenzlauer Berg in the borough of Pankow extends north-east of Mitte and is one of Berlin's prettiest districts. It escaped serious damage during the war and was spared post-war redevelopment. In GDR times it was the centre of alternative culture and a punk holdout but it has since been flooded with West German yuppies. 'Prenzlberg' is now more part of the establishment than an insider tip. Countless pubs, restaurants, cafés, galleries and little shops have created a day and nightlife scene unrivalled in the rest of Berlin. It has also become famous for being one of the few places in Germany that has had a baby boom in recent years. Originally an agricultural area on a

One of the few remaining unrestored façades in Prenzlauer Berg

plateau with windmills, Prenzlauer Berg was first developed during the second half of the 19th century. Beer had become a popular Berlin drink and several farmers set up breweries using local water wells. Most of the housing construction took place from 1889 to 1905 and followed the Hobrecht plan for the urban development of Berlin, drawn up in 1862 under King Friedrich Wilhelm IV. It was mostly paid for with the reparation money the French had to give the Prussians after the Franco-Prussian War and the Parisian feel to the area stems from the Prussian King's admiration for Hausmann's boulevards in the French capital.

Prenzlauer Berg was designed mainly as a working-class district. The rows of five-storey tenement buildings (Mietskasernen) usually have several backyards (Hinterhöfe) containing further blocks of flats with cramped living conditions and less light. Since 1990 these buildings have been gradually renovated and they make a magnificent sight up and down the broad tree-lined streets. Among the residential streets and squares are some architectural treasures, including several large churches. The best known is the Gethsemanekirche on Stargarder Straße whose dissident congregation played a crucial role in starting the 1989 revolution.

The Wasserturm (water tower) between Knaackstraße and Belforter Straße is a Prenzlauer Berg landmark nicknamed 'Dicker Hermann' (Fat

Water tower and park, Prenzlauer Berg

Hermann). It has a thinner, older brother where opponents of the Nazis were rounded up in 1933 and held in a machine house before being murdered. Inside the water reservoir is the eerie 'Singuhr Galerie' where sound-sculptures echo around the dark and empty brick interior of the historic water reservoirs. The apartments in the large tower were designed for the water tower workers and their families and are still in use today. There is a small park with trampolines and wild rabbits, well-loved by local families and restaurants with names like **Pasternak** and **Gagarin** are a reminder of Soviet sector days.

Another architectural highlight of Prenzlauer Berg is the **KulturBrauerei.** This former Schultheiß brewery complex built in1842 has been converted into a cultural centre and creative workplace. The brick buildings and cobbled streets form a great backdrop for the events staged here and the rest of the time people come to enjoy the cafés, clubs and cinema or to pick up walking or cycling tours. Almost next door is a family-run Italian restaurant, **Il Cenacolo**. The 'Kollwitzkiez' of Prenzlauer Berg is the area around Kollwitzplatz, a leafy square surrounded by apartment buildings, shops and restaurants. Named after artist Käthe Kollwitz who lived nearby, this was the secret meeting place for dissidents during the GDR era. Now the neighbourhood has a very established feel to it and there are some great restaurants

Small Worlds

and cafés. **Gugelhof** is where President Clinton dined when he visited Berlin and **Restauration 1900** existed in GDR days and retains pre-war ambience. Locals hang out at **Lafil** and **November** and love **Café Anna Blume, Sowohl als auch** and **Werkstatt der Süße** for coffee and cakes. **Café Chagall** near Senefelderplatz still reeks of pre-1989 days, but the Kiez classic is the **Metzer Eck,** an old Berlin corner pub that has hardly changed since 1913. The best time to be in Kollwitzplatz is on Saturdays when the market arrives and the local families are out in force. The square still has atmosphere, but the smell of revolution has long gone.

If you like the feel of the Kollwitzkiez, the Bötzowkiez on the other side of Greifswalder Straße has similar charm but is quieter. The M4 tram stops at the end of cobbled Hufelandstraße with its string of tempting shops and street cafés. **Kaffeeraum** makes a perfect coffee stop. For lunch or dinner **Alt Wien** or **Chez Maurice** are good choices. Start or end the evening at the **Saphire Bar** to lend a little elegance to life.

North of Danziger Straße is Helmholtzplatz, or 'Helmi' as it is known locally. This Kiez is edgier and attracts a younger crowd. Over the past few years millions of Euros have been pumped into renovations, pushing rents up and forcing out most of the original residents. The once punked-out, drug-strewn square of the 1990s has been relandscaped and cleaned up and the surrounding streets are full of treats. **Goldhahn and Sampson** is a great deli for foodies and there are lots of interesting shops and café stops. A good 'Helmikiez' choice for a relaxed café/bar experience is the **Wohnzimmer**. You can enjoy fondue at **Ars Vini,** top sushi at **Sasaya** and the **Weinschenke Weinstein** is popular for lunch or dinner. There is no shortage of late-night bars either, although some of them are now too commercialised. Cocktail connoisseurs should knock at **Becketts Kopf Bar.**

The centre of nightlife in Prenzlauer Berg is traditionally the area around Eberswalder Straße station. This is where young East Berliners used to meet under the U-Bahn arches and over half a century later it is still a cool Kiez. Kastanienallee is known as a hunting ground for trendy Berliners and international scene seekers and has earned the nickname 'Castingallee'; it is certainly a good place for a spot of people watching. The avenue takes its real name from the horse chestnut trees which were planted in 1826. It would be hard to create a consummate list of Kiez favourites in this area. It is a shifting scene, but some places have stood the test of time. Berlin's oldest beer garden, the **Prater Garten,** opened in 1853 is still going strong. **Konnopke's Imbiss** was started by 'motorbike Max' in 1930 and has become an East Berlin Currywurst legend. **An einem Sonntag im**

Husemannstraße, Prenzlauer Berg

August is grungy but well-located and **Café Morgenrot** is a Kiez institution. The staff at **I Due Forni** have punk attitude but the pizza is delicious. Shoppers wanting to escape chain stores will love Kastanienallee – there are countless fashion boutiques and small designer stores.

The prettiest street in this neighbourhood is Oderberger Straße. The elegant buildings have been beautifully renovated and in the summer sunshine nothing beats sitting at a table on the broad cobbled pavements. **Kauf dich Glücklich** is a unique mix of ice cream parlour and vintage junk store and **Rote Lotte** a neighbourhood bar more like a family living room. The western end of Oderberger Straße used to be blocked off by the Berlin Wall. After it fell, the one kilometre long strip of no man's land between Wedding and Prenzlauer Berg was turned into the aptly named Mauerpark. Locals now walk their dogs and sunbathe on land which was once heavily-mined and patrolled by armed guards. On Sundays the park turns into a vast flea market.

Friedrichshain

Friedrichshain to the east of Mitte has been officially amalgamated with Kreuzberg on the other side of the Spree, a district with a very different postwar history. Separated for 28 years by the Berlin Wall, Friedrichshain and

Kreuzberg are both full of urban buzz and diversity. A bit run-down in places, Friedrichshain was the last area to be cleared of squatters and is still the focal point for Berlin's left-wing anarchist scene. It is an intriguing mixture of concrete socialist high-rises, monumental Stalin-era mammoths and stylish, late-19th century town houses. Karl-Marx-Allee is the main architectural feature of Friedrichshain. This showcase avenue, originally called Stalinallee, was created in 1949 as a birthday present for Stalin. The spacious flats were highly prized in GDR times and there is still a faint whiff of socialist utopia in the air. On the main avenue shops and restaurants have sprung up which belong to the era of post-Wall capitalism. **Café Sibylle** has a small exhibition on the history of Karl-Marx-Allee, **Café Henselmann** is run by the granddaughter of the architect who designed the grand Moscow-style buildings and **Café Alberts** is a lively meeting place for locals. The classic GDR evening venues were the **Kino International**, the **Kosmos** or **Café Moskau** but the new scene has taken root around Weberwiese station. Here you can find the hip **CSA Bar** and the trendy **Sanatorium 23.**

To the north of Karl-Marx-Allee near Straußberger Platz is Volkspark Friedrichshain, opened in 1848 as the eastern alternative to the Tiergarten. In summer it is packed with locals lazing by the lake or sitting on the terrace of **Café Schoenbrunn**. At dusk the atmosphere in the beer garden hots up and the Freiluftkino (open-air cinema) attracts large audiences. The fabulous Märchenbrunnen (fairy tale fountain) is a popular meeting point. Built in 1913 it is decorated with sculptures of characters invented by the Brothers Grimm who settled in Berlin. The most important memorial in the park is the 'Friedhof der Märzgefallenen', a small cemetery for the hundreds of victims who died at the barricades in the 1848 revolution and the November revolution of 1918.

At Frankfurter Tor, Friedrichshain divides into north and south. To the north is Bersarinplatz with traces of the old squatters' scene and leading off it are two very contrasting streets. Bänschstraße is known for its beautifully restored Art Nouveau architecture and Rigaer Straße for its vocal punk population. But if you head south down Warschauer Straße, you will come to the part of Friedrichshain that gives this district its cool reputation. At night the Simon-Dach-Straße is packed with party-goers and by day this old working-class Kiez now has a bohemian feel to it. In the 1990s students moved into the old tenement buildings because rents were cheap but now wealthier residents occupy the ones that have been renovated. On Sundays there is a popular flea market at **Boxhagener Platz.** Recommended places for a good Berlin brunch are **Café Datscha** or **Volckswirtschaft** or for coffe and cake

Märchenbrunnen, Friedrichshain

try **Kaffeeladen** or **Cupcake**. To discover authentic, uncommercialised Friedrichshain, wander over to the picturesque Knorrpromenade and a little further east Sonntagstraße by the Ostkreuz station is a Kiez that hasn't been discovered by the rest of the world.

Kreuzberg

This former West Berlin borough features the idyllic Landwehrkanal, an inner-city waterway, designed by Lenné and completed in 1850 to link Berlin with Köpenick. Kreuzberg is well-known as the place where thousands of Turkish immigrants and free thinkers settled during the city's division. Surrounded on two sides by the Wall, there was little investment in the infrastructure and rents remained cheap. Young men flooded in from West Germany to avoid compulsory military service, punks squatted in abandoned houses and the gay community found a liberal environment. In recent years dot-coms, marketing agencies and the wealthy middle classes have moved into renovated lofts and apartments and there are now two distinct types of Kreuzberg Kiez – the wild 36 and the tame 61 districts, numbers which originate from former Berlin postcodes. There's a saying that "the guy from 61 drives a Mercedes, and the guy from 36 rips off its emblem".

Kreuzberg 36, north of the Landwehrkanal, is known for its May Day riots, now an annual ritual in the German capital. So many Turkish families live in the area around Kottbusser Tor station that it is often called 'Little Istanbul' and the U-Bahn line 1 has been dubbed the 'Orient Express'. Walking through colourful Oranienstraße you could almost be in Turkey, if the kebab joints, bazaars and coffee houses weren't regularly interspersed with clubs, bars and trendy little shops. There were once small mosques in courtyards behind the shops, but the opening of the grand Omar Ibn Al-Khattab mosque in May 2010 has brought the Turkish community into the 21st century. It was at **Hasir's** on Adalbertstraße that the traditional Döner Kebab ('Iskender') meal was turned into fast food by putting it into pitta bread. **Mercan** near Görlitzer station is also a great place for an authentic Turkish meal. But for pre-war Berlin surroundings the best tips are **Die Henne** and **Max und Moritz.**

On Tuesdays and Fridays the locals head for the **Maybachufer Turkish Market**, along the southern bank of the Landwehrkanal. This takes place just outside Kreuzberg in the district of Neukölln, often referred to as 'Kreuzkölln'. On the Paul-Lincke-Ufer is the upmarket **Horvath** (formerly **Exil,** where Bowie partied and Warhol painted) and further along is the laid-back **Senti** tapas bar and restaurant. A large synagogue once stood on Fraenkelufer in the 'Urbanhafen' area. Now on summer nights a kind of Woodstock aura develops on the Admiralbrücke when large crowds gather to watch the sunset. If **Il Casolare** gets too full there are several restaurant boats nearby and the **Brachvogel** has a beer garden and mini-golf.

Mariannenkiez is another interesting neighbourhood in Kreuzberg 36. At its centre is Mariannenplatz, a pretty mid-19th century square. On one side is the **Bethanien**, a complex of buildings with a fascinating history. Originally built as a hospital in 1845, it was abandoned in 1970 and used by squatters. Since then the main building has housed social projects, an avant-garde cultural centre and now the **3 Schwestern** restaurant with high ceilings and a magical garden. In summer the Kreuzberg open-air cinema shows films in English in the Bethanien's grounds. East of Kottbusser Tor is the Wrangelkiez, one of Berlin's most vibrant neigbourhoods. At weekends it can become overwhelmed with clubbers, but still has charm and an anarchic cheerfulness. The **Weltrestaurant Markthalle** next to the old market hall is a great Kiez experience; a friendly pub restaurant with chunky wooden tables and a 'Privatklub' in the basement for fans of the genuine German cellar bar. Other local tips are the Moroccan restaurant **Baraka, La Buvette**, an interesting new bistro and the **Kimchi Princess**, a Korean bar-

Inside the Künstlerhaus Bethanien, Kreuzberg

becue restaurant. Görlitzer Park is the cultural junction for many Kreuzbergers, the site of a former railway terminus and now a run-down park. In summer there is a regular team of frisbee-throwers and flame-jugglers, barbecues go on long into the night and occasional raves occupy the park's lower end. Activities are centred round a crater which was once the old station's subway and the café/club **Das Edelweiss** in the old station building (the name refers to the station's heritage as Berlin's first connection to Vienna).

Moving westwards into Kreuzberg '61' the atmosphere is more restrained. The Graefekiez is a neighbourhood between the Landwehrkanal and the Volkspark Hasenheide. With Graefestraße at its heart, this Kiez is full of tiny cafés and tempting shops. **Fuchsbau** is the hangout for the cool crowd and **King of Falafel** is true to its name. Still further west is the exalted Bergmannkiez, which includes the streets between Yorkstraße, Gneisenaustraße, Bergmannstraße and Viktoria Park. It has a Mediterranean feel in summer and is populated with the wealthier end of the alternative scene. Most of the buildings were spared destruction during the war-time bombing, partly due to their proximity to Tempelhof airport. Chamissoplatz is the architectural highlight. Cobbled streets and 19th century town houses surround a small park with a perfectly restored example of a 'Café Achteck' (literally meaning octagon café), the name given to the traditional Berlin urinals. On Saturdays the residents turn out for their farmers' market and in the evenings repair to the corner pub **G wie Gulasch**. There are some excellent eateries along Bergmannstraße. **Knofi, s'Hegeles Teufelsküche, Bar Centrale** and **Felix Austria** and **Barcomi's Deli** are all favourites. **Marheineke Markthalle** is one of the last indoor market halls in Berlin, renovated in 2007. Much of the atmosphere was lost in the process, but the new building is well laid-out and there are colourful stalls selling organic produce and eco-friendly products, as well as lunch bars.

Viktoria Park attracts a broader spectrum of Kreuzbergers. Guitar-wielding, dope-smoking hippies sit under the trees, groups of young Turks kick a football about on the lawns and sporty forty-somethings jog past groups of young mothers pushing their strollers along the path. This park is on the slopes of the 66 metre high Kreuzberg, the hill that gave its name to the surrounding area. The summit is crowned with an ornate Schinkel monument commemorating the Wars of Liberation and the views across Berlin are splendid. Viktoria Park is a great place to go at dusk before an evening exploring the nightlife in the streets below. The hub of all the action in summer is **Golgatha,** both day and night. If you prefer something quieter, **Osteria No1** has a pretty courtyard and good Italian food. Whilst in the area you shouldn't miss the beautifully restored **Riehmers Hofgarten**, an estate built for Prussian army officers at the end of the 19th century and an example of inspired city planning and architecture. After a stroll through the historic cobbled streets, you could head off to the **Yorkschlösschen**, a 100 year old Kreuzberg institution and Berlin's 'home of jazz and blues', or complete the Kreuzberg experience with a visit to **Curry 36,** the famous Currywurst stand on Mehringdamm.

Neukölln

This gritty, 'multi-kulti' borough has long been home to squatters, artist and musicians and has a claim to fame as a track on Bowie's 'Heroes' album (1977). These days Neukölln's raw edge has softened and it has become a Berlin cultural hotspot. The rents are cheap, transport links are good and a creative younger crowd has moved in and altered the social dynamics. Just inside Neukölln along the Maybachufer is the Turkish market and every third Sunday a flea market dubbed the 'Nowkoelln Flowmarkt'. There are also a number of lively cafés and bars, such as **Der Silberlöffel** and **Nansen**.

Neuköllner Oper

The centre of Neukölln is around Karl-Marx-Straße, a working-class high street experiencing a cultural renaissance. This area was once the town of Rixdorf and the 'Saalbau' building, opened in 1876, became a renowned Berlin theatre. It fell into neglect for many years but was reopened in 1990 as a cultural centre. The theatre was renamed Heimathafen and in a courtyard behind it is the cool **Café Rix**, a former dance hall decorated with golden stucco, and large, gilt-edged mirrors. Only a few doors down the road is the ballroom of Rixdorf's former reception hall, where every year the **Neuköllner Oper** stages a dozen or so interesting operas.

Another Neukölln highlight is its **Puppentheater-Museum** with a collection of over 300 different puppets in a glass-roofed former sculptor's studio. The **s…kultur** restaurant in Neukölln's Rathaus does a great deal for lunch and is a beacon of social integration. Breakfast is best at **Rudimarie** and local vegetarians love **Der Kleine Buddha.** Neuköllners also recommend **Mariamulata** and **Jimmy Woo.**

The oldest and prettiest part of Neukölln is Alt-Rixdorf. In 1737, King Frederick William I of Prussia allowed about 350 Moravian Protestants expelled from Bohemia to settle here and along Kirchgasse as far as Richardplatz are the remains of this Bohemian village, with its winding streets, small houses and courtyards. Other attractions include the Comenius Garden, the 15th century Bethlehemkirche, the working Dorfschmiede (village smithy), St. Magdalene's Church and the Bohemian Museum in the old schoolhouse. Join the locals of Alt-Rixdorf at **Louis** on Richardplatz for the biggest Wiener Schnitzel in Berlin.

Schöneberg

Schöneberg literally means 'lovely hill' and is a West Berlin district with great style. This part of the city was generally not heavily bombed, so it gives a good idea of what pre-war Berlin looked like. In the mid-19th century, Berliners came to Schöneberg to dance and party. When Schöneberg became part of Greater Berlin after the First World War, the gay and lesbian district around Nollendorfplatz was a big part of the 'Goldene Zwanziger' (the Roaring Twenties), with hip establishments offering debauchery and experimental theatre. Then the Nazis came and switched off the lights. Writer Christopher Isherwood lived at 17 Nollendorfstraße and the musical and film 'Cabaret' are based on his pre-war experiences here. In the West Berlin of the 70s and 80s Schöneberg's nightlife scene had a big revival and some of these bars where David Bowie used to hang out are still going strong. The gay scene also continues to thrive, especially on Motzstraße and Fuggerstraße and many of the fashionable shops survived both the fall of the Wall and the rise of the ultra trendy districts in Mitte and Prenzlauer Berg. Less hectic is the area around picturesque Viktoria-Luise-Platz where you can easily while away an hour or so in one of the pavement cafés.

The classic downtown Schöneberg tour starts at Nollendorfplatz along Maaßenstraße, past **Berio, Nachbar, Amrit, Slumberland, Impala** and **Habibi**, all buzzing with locals, depending on the time of day. On Winterfeldtplatz there is a market on Wednesdays and Saturdays where you can see the entire range of Schönebergers out in force. Behind the tall Catholic St Matthias Church is Goltzstraße with specialist shops selling original shoes and clothes and irresistible junk and retro items. Stop off at **Mister Hu** for a cocktail or **TeeTeaThe** for something more sedate. Akazienstraße is another lively Kiez. **Romantica** and **Renger Patzsch** are two restaurant recommendations and **Gottlob** is the locals' favourite for a great value set lunch. **Bilderbuch** ('Picture Book') is the perfect place to hang out at any time of day, but if you are just passing through, **Double Eye** serves top coffee. There are lots of pretty shops too, selling everything from books to bags and hats to herbs. The trendy Schöneberg scene seems to end at Hauptstraße, but there is much more to discover nearby. On Potsdamer Straße are the grand colon-

Viktoria-Luise-Platz, Schöneberg

nades of the Kleistpark containing the Kammergericht (Superior Court of Justice). During the Nazi dictatorship this building housed the notorious Volksgerichtshof (People's Court) and after the war it was occupied first by the Allied Control Council and then the Berlin Air Safety Centre. The park itself started out as the Berlin Botanical Gardens and the original Botanical Museum and Herbarium was in Haus am Kleistpark, now the borough's cultural centre. Only a short walk from Kleistpark is a Schöneberg Kiez untainted by the kind of urban cleansing experienced in the Akazienkiez. Langenscheidtstraße leads to Crellestraße, both streets with faded elegance and interesting shopfronts. Locals hang out in **Toronto** and children play by the fountain. A strong social conscience is evident too. Behind ground-floor windows classrooms of immigrant women are being taught German.

Marlene Dietrich, the famous German singer and actress was born in 1901 in a Schöneberg neighbourhood known as the Rote Insel ('Red Island'), a triangle-shaped area enclosed by S-Bahn tracks across the railway bridge on Großgörschenstraße. Before the end of World War I half the Island's territory was used by the Prussian Army and the other half was a working-class residential district, dominated by voters of left-wing 'red' parties. These days the Rote Insel has an ethnically diverse population and an unobtrusive bohemian charm. The Alter St Matthäus-Kirchhof, a cemetery created in

1856, is filled with opulent gravestones and memorials of the 19th century Berlin bourgeoisie. Celebrities buried here include the Brothers Grimm and a memorial tombstone honours von Stauffenberg and his fellow conspirators in the July 1944 plot. The Königin-Luise-Gedächtniskirche between Leberstraße (Dietrich was born at number 65) and Naumannstraße is an unusual round church with seven doors. After dark, check out the cocktails at the **Jansen Bar** round the corner on Gotenstraße.

Although Marlene Dietrich left for Hollywood in 1930, became an American citizen and sang for the American troops during the war, she wanted to be buried in Berlin. Her much-visited grave is in the Städtischer Friedhof III, on Stubenrauchstraße in the Schöneberg district of Friedenau. The cottage-style Friedenau station is surrounded by several good cafés and the fine buildings in this leafy suburb date from the Gründerzeit and Jugendstil (Art Nouveau) periods. Many authors, painters, philosophers and writers have found inspiration here and the **Literatur Hotel** on Fregestraße hosts readings by current Berlin authors in the exquisite Uwe Johnson room.

The most famous of all buildings in Schöneberg is its Rathaus (Town Hall) where John F. Kennedy made his historic speech in 1963. This was West Berlin's main town hall during the Cold War and the Liberty Bell, a gift from the American people, as well as other memorabilia from that era are on display here. On 9th November 1989, Chancellor Helmut Kohl and Willy Brandt stood on the main balcony and waved at the crowds celebrating the fall of the Berlin Wall. On the western edge of Schöneberg is Tauentzienstraße and the grand **KaDeWe** department store where on Saturday mornings the wealthier Schönebergers can be found brunching in style in the 6th Floor Food Hall. If it gets too crowded, a great alternative nearby is the beautifully-restored art deco Ellington Hotel, whose **Duke** restaurant has an in-house jazz radio station.

The 'High'light of Schöneberg is its 80 metre high historic gas holder. Well-trained guides lead small groups of visitors up the 456 steps for a spectacular panorama of the city and an explanation of the view. Tours can be booked at www.climb-berlin.com.

Charlottenburg-Wilmersdorf

Charlottenburg with its main boulevard, the Kurfürstendamm, is the epitome of a particular image of Berlin – cosmopolitan, bohemian and elegant. For American writer Thomas Wolfe the Ku'damm of the 1920s was 'Europe's biggest café'. But Charlottenburg was also a fine residential address and

Café Bleibtreu, Charlottenburg

some of the evidence is still there to see. When Berlin was divided, Charlottenburg and Wilmersdorf were in the British sector and formed the centre of West Berlin. Apartment blocks and department stores sprang up and the restored Ku'damm area enjoyed a post-war revival, largely subsidised by West Germany. In 1989 the fall of the Berlin Wall changed all this. The new building projects shifted everything east and the old West Berlin began to look rather tawdry. The centre of Charlottenburg fell into the hands of new Russian money and became known as 'Charlottograd'. Over the past few years it has put on some style, reasserted itself as a place to be seen and there are great neighbourhoods to discover.

The Ku'damm itself has wonderful shops and famous cafés like **Kempinski Eck** and **Café Kranzler** but you need to get off the main avenue to get a feel for the authentic Charlottenburg scene. The refined **Café Literaturhaus** on Fasanenstraße attracts the intelligentsia and **Meineke X** on Meinekestraße is an authentic old pub with Berlin specialities. Bleibtreustraße has smart boutiques and several feel-good restaurants in all price ranges. The **Café Bleibtreu** does a great line in brunches and for a traditional Berlin experience try the **Zillemarkt** just in front of the railway bridge. Under the bridge on the right is Savignypassage, which leads past the arches S-Bahn arches to Savignyplatz, the focal point of Charlottenburg's reputation as a district for artists and intellectuals. Restaurants, street cafés and bars surround the gardens of this pretty 1920s square on both sides of Kantstraße. **Café Brel** and **mr hai & Friends** get top marks with locals, **Gainsbourg** is a bar with French soul and the **Hefner Lounge** is the place for chilling. On Kantstraße, the legendary **Paris Bar** still has cachet and the wonderful **Schwarzes Café** stays open all night. For a genuine Berlin 'Kneipe' with local colour and colourful locals, try the **Dicke Wirtin** or the **Zwiebelfisch**. Just around the corner is the excellent **Florian** restaurant and the venerable **A-Trane** Jazz bar.

North of Savignyplatz around Goethestraße are some of the most attractive streets in Charlottenburg. This is still a thriving community and the specialist shops and cafés are always busy, especially on Saturday. Kantstraße has plenty on offer too, including several shops with good interior design ideas, especially the vast **Stilwerk**. The **Bücherbögen** under the railway arches at Savignyplatz stocks a wide choice of arty books and **Marga Schoeller** on Knesebeckstraße has a huge selection of English books. Mommsenstraße is full of eye-catching façades, little front gardens and interesting doorways. You can be enticed into buying pretty antiques and designer second-hand clothes or enjoy an East Prussian meal at **Marjellchen.**

Walter-Benjamin-Platz, the large piazza off Wielandstraße, has a special atmosphere in the sunshine. Lunch al fresco at **Il Calice** or relax in a beach basket chair at **Silber Antik**. Further along Giesebrechtstraße are several well-established Berlin institutions. The **Mommseneck** has been going since 1905 and boasts 100 different bottled beers. Next door is the authentic **Café Richter,** an insider tip for breakfast, coffee and cakes. The **Kurpfalz Weinstuben**, tucked away behind modern shops on Adenauerplatz is a true survivor of the bombing. Now in its 75th year this historic family-run wine bar has candlelit cellar-style rooms – a must for fans of the Heimat films. Avoid the Wilmersdorfer shopping precinct behind Charlottenburg station and make for Stuttgarter Platz under the spreading chestnut trees. The cafés that sprawl around 'Stutti' are full of regulars and the surrounding area is criss-crossed with wide tree-lined cobbled streets, some with shops and cafés on the ground floor of the substantial Charlottenburg apartment blocks. Leonhardtstraße has most on offer and Suarezstraße is known among Berliners for its antique shops. Here are two more local treasures, **Stella Alpina**, a well-loved Italian restaurant and the pretty **Wald Königsberger** home-made marzipan shop.

Charlottenburg is also renowned for its beautiful palace, park and museums. Once you have explored its cultural heritage, venture further

Stuttgarter Platz, Windscheidstraße, Charlottenburg

down Schloßstraße to find a table in one of the garden cafés half-hidden behind the hedges. **Restaurant Lietzenburg** is an oasis of calm. On the other side of the Kaiserdamm is the urban retreat of Lietzensee. There is a path all around the lake where weeping willows dip into the water and in autumn the colours of the parkland trees are stunning. **Engelbecken** or **Manstein** are popular meeting places and the friendly **Stattcafé** at the southern end is only a few minutes from quite a different walk through nature. Find your way to 29 Rönnestraße, open the metal gate and walk through the tunnel to the magic land of summer gardens on railway sidings that belonged to the Reichsbahn in GDR days.

In the evening Pariser Straße and Ludwigkirchstraße on the Wilmersdorf side of the Ku'damm are full of well-established bars and restaurants. Uhlandstraße has plenty on offer too and **Rum Trader** on the corner of Fasanenstraße is a gem of a Berlin cocktail bar, a perfect setting for Hemingway. But the most picturesque setting in this area is Ludwigkirchplatz, where **Weyers** restaurant is the favourite with local residents. For later in the evening try the **al2 Cocktailbar** or one of the dance bars along Pariser Straße. Back on the Ku'damm there is a popular **Zeitlos** bar and the **Universum Lounge**, whose space-age design signals Charlottenburg's resolve to be a main player in 21st century Berlin.

The Outer Edges

Berlin spreads out graciously across its twelve boroughs in a city nine times the size of Paris. But it is not just urban sprawl. If you fly over Berlin on a cloudless day you will be struck by the vast amount of forests and parks, lakes and rivers. It is all easily accessible by public transport, provided you have equipped yourself with a good map.

NORTH
Alt-Tegel

Tegel is not just the name of an airport. It is a district of Berlin with large expanses of forest, lakes and pretty countryside. There's an old Berlin rhyme which goes: 'Mit Kind und Kegel, auf nach Tegel!' loosely meaning 'take the whole family off to Tegel'. This is exactly what Berliners have been doing for centuries. Alt-Tegel station is the best starting point for exploring the area. It's short walk down to the Tegeler See where you can enjoy the lake from the Greenwich-Promenade, featuring an old red British post box and telephone kiosk, or take a boat trip from one of the piers.

Tegel Forest

Alt-Heiligensee, an old fishing village with a historic church and pretty cottages, is only 15 minutes on the 113 bus from Alt-Tegel. From here, take the 324 bus as far as the Rallenweg stop. The walk back to the Greenwich Promenade through the Tegel forest, with its spectacularly tall trees, takes about an hour and a half. After crossing the Konradshöher Straße you soon come to the northernmost tip of the Tegler See. Standing by the lake near the **Waldhütte** café is the oldest tree in Berlin, a 900 year old oak tree christened 'Dicke Marie' by the famous Humboldt brothers who grew up in nearby Schloss Tegel and named the tree after their cook, 'fat Mary'.

Lübars

The 222 bus from Alt-Tegel station to the village of Alt-Lübars takes half an hour. The route runs parallel to the 'Barnimer Dörferweg', a footpath through the meadows of the Tegeler Fließ which flows into the lake at Tegel. Alt-Lübars is on the borders of Berlin and Brandenburg, where West Berlin used to be just a few metres from the border with East Germany. The Wall and the watch towers have long gone and now there are no Allied patrols to intrude on the peaceful scene of village green, church, farmhouses and cottages. Next to the old village inn, the **Alter Dorfkrug Lübars**, is a reconstruction of an original village hut and a map showing all the local walks.

Pankow

Schloss Schönhausen, a baroque Hohenzollern palace in the borough of Pankow, has a fascinating history. From 1740 to 1797 Frederick the Great exiled his estranged wife here and these same rooms were used as offices for the GDR's first president, Wilhelm Pieck in the 1950s. The palace later became a state guesthouse and received several famous political leaders including Indira Gandhi, Fidel Castro and the Gorbachevs. After the GDR's demise, the so-called 'round-table discussions' that paved the way to German reunification took place here. The splendid interior has now been meticulously restored and is well worth a visit. The river Panke meanders through the palace grounds designed by Lenné as an English landscape and there are pretty walks along the river bank. Not far from the palace is the Majakowskiring where many of the top-ranking East German politcians used to live until 1990. Most of the houses were built in the 1920s as private mansions and were expropriated after the war. The **Gasthaus Majakowski** restaurant is a revelation – an aristocratic setting in a socialist stronghold. The M1 tram or bus 50 takes you back to Pankow station.

EAST
Alt-Köpenick

Alt-Köpenick boasts a long history and a magical setting on the rivers Spree and Dahme. Take bus 164 or tram 68 from Köpenick S-Bahn station to the Rathaus (Town Hall), famed for the story of one of its citizens. In 1906, a shoemaker dressed up as an army captain, imprisoned the mayor, took over the town hall, stole the city treasury and was immortalised by Carl Zuck-

Rathaus Köpenick

mayer in his play 'Der Hauptmann von Köpenick' (1931). The Rathaus has a traditional **Ratskeller**, a cellar restaurant with vaulted ceilings. It's worth exploring the streets of the old town and the historic waterside **Waschhaus** inn does a good Sunday brunch.

Schloss Köpenick is a Hohenzollern palace built in 1677–85 in Dutch baroque style. It is surrounded by water and gardens and forms part of Berlin's Applied Arts Museum. The exhibition rooms have fabulous stucco work and ceiling frescoes and the 'Wappensaal' with its display of Hohenzollern porcelain and silver is amazing. It was in the armoury here that a court martial sentenced the crown prince Friedrich (later Frederick the Great) and his friend Lieutenant von Katte for their planned escape to England. Frederick's father made him witness von Katte's execution.

Müggelsee and Müggelberge

Köpenick is also the gateway to East Berlin's lakes and forests. Here the River Spree opens out into a huge lake surrounded by thick woodland and the highest natural hills in Berlin. Take the S-Bahn out to Köpenick, then bus X69 towards Odernheimer Straße. On the right are the wooded hills of the Müggelberge and on the left, behind tall trees, the wide waters of the Großer

Müggelsee. At the Rübezahl bus stop there are two choices – the hills or the lake. The Müggelturm on the 88 metre high 'Kleiner Müggelberg' gives a stunning panoramic view. On the western horizon is the Fernsehturm and the city centre and to the east 'Tropical Islands', Europe's largest indoor tropical holiday resort. The 'Großer Müggelberg' is the highest hill (115 metres) and it is 374 steps down to the Langer See. There is a pretty lakeside walk past the Grünau rowing regatta course used for the 1936 Berlin Olympics. When you reach Wendenschloss you can either return to Köpenick on the 62 tram or take the ferry over to Grünau.

A walk around the southern side of Großer Müggelsee to Friedrichshagen can either start at Rübezahl or you can add on a mile or so by taking the X69 as far as Odernheimer Straße. At Rübezahl there is a beer garden by the water's edge with boats to hire and from here the path becomes more crowded. The Spreetunnel, 80 years old and 120 metres long, leads into Friedrichshagen, an historic resort whose famous landmark is the tall chimney of the Berliner Bürgerbräu, the oldest Berlin brewery still in operation. The brewery has a waterside restaurant or there is **Die Weisse Villa** – both have fabulous views. Trams 60 and 61 both run to Friedrichshagen station or it is a short walk back along Bölschestraße with its mix of architecture stretching back over 250 years.

Tram 68 is one of the prettiest tram routes in Germany. It runs between Köpenick station and Alt-Schmöckwitz and after crossing the river Dahme begins its magical woodland and lakeside journey. In the summer months a ferry plies across the Langer See from Zum Seeblick in Schmökwitz over to Krampenburg. From here there is a riverside walk by the Große Krampe to Müggelheim where you can pick up the X69 back to Köpenick. Alternatively, just cross over the Schmökwitzer bridge and either stroll down to the beach bar on the right or turn left for a walk along the bank of the Seddinsee. This path soon leads to the **Strandlust**, a restaurant on a converted barge.

Ahrensfelder Berge

This insider tip is for adventurous visitors, interested in unusual views and perspectives. The Ahrensfelde Hills are in the East Berlin outer borough of Marzahn-Hellersdorf and can be reached by tram M6 to Betriebshof Marzahn. They are 112 and 101 metres high and look over to the Brandenburg countryside to the north and the East Berlin urban and industrial landscape to the south. This is where the GDR built huge socialist housing estates around the village of Alt-Marzahn, which bizarrely still exists, together with

Botanischer Garten, Steglitz

its windmill. The steps up to the top of the hills are especially atmospheric and the urban views are unique.

SOUTH

Parks and Gardens

South Berlin's green lungs consist of wonderful parks and gardens. Der 'Botanische Garten' (Botanic Gardens) in Dahlem, home of the West Berlin Freie Universität (Free University), is only three stops on the M48 bus from Rathaus Steglitz. This is one of the largest botanical gardens in the world with an extravagant wealth of plant life in themed gardens and huge, magnificent greenhouses.

Bus 170 from Rathaus Steglitz runs eastward across a large section of South Berlin, like a magical mystery tour of green areas. First stop is the 78 metre high 'Insulaner', a hill made of rubble. There is a planetarium, outdoor swimming pool and mini-golf on offer or you can walk over to Priesterweg and discover the 'Natur-Park Schöneberger Südgelände'. After the war the Tempelhof railway sidings were gradually shut down and in just 50 years a diverse, species-rich natural oasis has developed here. Some of the tracks, relics and buildings dating back to the railway era are dotted among the wild

Britzer Garten

grassland and jungle and the locomotive hall has become a creative space. Change buses to the M44 at Britzer Damm/Gradestraße and you will arrive at the main entrance of the **Britzer Garten**, created in 1985 as the Federal Garden Show and now a beautifully-kept site with changing landscapes and flower displays throughout the year. There are lakeside cafés, a windmill and a tourist train. If you stay on the 170, the route continues across the Teltow Canal and past little garden colonies whose names sum up their purpose. Who could resist spending sunny weekends in 'Happy Harmony', 'Red Sunset' or 'No Worries'? When the bus reaches Späthstraße you are not far from Baumschulenweg, a whole area of Berlin devoted to plant and tree nurseries set up by the Späth gardening dynasty in 1720. In 1874 Franz Späth built a family mansion and planted a stunning arboretum with over a thousand exotic trees. The Späth-Arboretum is now run by the Humboldt University Botany Department and is open to the public in the summer. On the other side of Königsweg there are pretty walks through the Königsweide, once part of the large forest area south-east of Berlin.

To return to the city centre take the 170 bus as far as Baumschulenweg station or continue two more stops to the end of the route at the ferry that crosses the Spree. If you turn left along Kiehnwerderallee there's a surreal surprise in store – the abandoned **Spreepark**, a former GDR amusement

Courtyard of Jagdschloss Grunewald, Zehlendorf

park complete with big wheel, roller coaster, model dinosaurs and a colorful history. The Spree comes into view again at the end of Poetensteig and on sunny days the river is packed with boats of all shapes and sizes. This area is full of interest and has long been a favourite outing for East Berlin families. You can walk over the bridge to the idyllically situated Insel Berlin or explore the vast **Soviet War Memorial** in Treptower Park (page 200). The nearest station is Treptower Park.

WEST

The Grunewald

In the 16th century Elector Joachim II stocked this immense tract of 'green forest' with wild boar and deer and built himself a splendid Renaissance hunting lodge, the **Jagdschloss Grunewald**. In the aftermath of the war many of the pine trees in the Grunewald were used as firewood, but now it's a wonderful mixed forest of pines, beech, birch, oak and ash, criss-crossed with dappled paths and containing a series of lakes, secluded beaches, nature trails and historic inns. Since the war it has also acquired the Teufelsberg, an 80 metre high grassed-over hill of rubble, with great views from the top. During the Cold War the US National Security Agency built a large listening station

The wide waters of the Havel

on top of the hill. This eerie abandoned site is fenced off, but is a popular place for illegal parties, vandalism, graffiti and shooting films.

The walk from Grunewald station through the forest to the peaceful waters of the Grunewaldsee only takes about 20 minutes and is well signposted. The Jagdschloss has been beautifully renovated and has a fine collection of portrait paintings. There is a café in the courtyard and just south of the lake is the **Forsthaus Paulsborn**, a traditional restaurant with terrace. U-Bahn line 3 also takes you deep into the Grunewald, to the shores of two more pretty lakes. From Onkel Toms Hütte it's about half a mile to a woodland path leading to Krumme Lanke, a boomerang-shaped lake surrounded by thick woodland and with several swimming areas ('Badestellen'). At the end of it lie the even clearer waters of the Schlachtensee and between the two lakes stands the **Alte Fischerhütte**, once the stables where Frederick the Great made regular stops on his way from Berlin to Potsdam. The Schlachtensee has paths on both sides of the lake and there are beaches and boats for hire. A turning into the woodland leads back to Nikolassee station across Spanische Allee and over the Avus, originally a motor racing track but now part of the motorway. Von Stauffenberg lived with his brother at 8–10 Tristanstraße in Nikolassee at the time of the July Plot. He would meet up with other conspirators by the small lake among the dark trees.

The western edges of the Grunewald are bordered by the wide river Havel which opens out into the Wannsee lake. Bus 218 is a popular route on summer weekends and runs from Theodor-Heuss-Platz as far as Wannsee station. About halfway along is the Grunewaldturm with good views across the Havel landscape. More intrepid walkers can take the high road, the 'Havelhöhenweg' as far as the Wannsee lake.

The district of Grunewald includes the 'Villa-Kolonie' at the western end of the Ku'damm, built in Bismarck's day. The M19 bus runs through the heart of this elegant, leafy suburb with avenues full of large mansions. It was on Königsallee that the Foreign Minister of Germany Walther Rathenau was assassinated by right wing radicals on 22nd June 1922. A memorial stone marks the scene of the crime on a bend in the road. For a taste of Grunewald grandeur, explore the area around Douglasstraße, admire the chocolate-box views of Hundekehlesee and then enjoy lunch or tea in the elegant surroundings of **Reinhard's Landhaus**.

Wannsee

Wannsee is a lakeside resort only half an hour from the city centre, well-signposted from Nikolassee station. **Strandbad Wannsee** was originally opened in 1907 and is the largest inland beach in Europe. These days it has rather lost its pre-war glamour, but is still popular with Berliners and has every beach facility imaginable. There are boat excursions from Wannsee Bridge opposite Wannsee station or you can cross the lake using your train ticket on the BVG ferry over to Kladow. The trip takes 20 minutes and ferries run hourly. A pretty path, the 'Westliches Havelufer', runs along the west bank of the Havel and then through parkland and woodland up to the 134 bus route linking Spandau with Alt-Kladow. Or you can just settle for one of the beer gardens next to the pier.

A short walk from Wannsee station, on the other side of Königsstraße and a little way along Bismarckstraße by the Kleiner Wannsee, is a simple gravestone which marks the spot where the famous Romantic German writer, Heinrich von Kleist, committed suicide with Henriette Vogel on 21st November 1811. The two lovers sat down at a garden table they had brought with them and drank coffee, wine and rum. Then the writer took out two pistols from the picnic basket, shot Henriette in the chest and put the other pistol in his mouth. The Nazis replaced the New Testament inscription on the gravestone with a quote from one of Kleist's plays, "Nun, O Unsterblichkeit, bist du ganz mein." (Now, oh immortality, you are all mine).

Wirtshaus Moorlake, Wannsee

There are several bus excursions from Wannsee Station. Bus 114 takes you to the **Liebermann Villa** with its exhibition of paintings and beautiful gardens. It's a cruel irony that this eminent Jewish artist's lakeside home is so close to the notorious **Haus der Wannsee-Konferenz**, where the Nazis decided on the fate of European Jewry. Between these two historic mansions is the Heckeshorn promenade dominated by a huge zinc lion commemorating the Danish victory over the North Germans in 1850. There's a pretty yacht marina on the lake below and several eating places. **Bolles Bootshaus** is popular for barbecues on summer weekends.

The 218 bus links up with the two minute ferry trip across to **Pfaueninsel** (Peacock Island). This Prussian Arcadia is one of Berlin's most magical gardens. The island's landscape was designed by Lenné at the end of the 18th century as a romantic hideaway for Friedrich Wilhelm II and his mistress. This king died prematurely after being hit in the eye with a champagne cork and his successor, Friedrich Wilhelm III, sad widower of Luise, stocked it with a great variety of exotic animals, including the peacocks that still patrol the green lawns. The island is full of idiosyncrasies; the ruined medieval white castle is a sham and the mock-gothic farm has real geese. It is also a protected nature reserve so there are no cafés or bicycles. It would take about three hours to cover everything, but it is worth walking to the Luisen-

Schloss Glienicke, Wannsee

tempel at the end of the island and then back along the water's edge to the ferry. On the mainland the **Wirtshaus zur Pfaueninsel** serves as a good refreshment stop.

Two paths from here both end at **Schloss Glienicke**, another Prussian paradise. The upper path leads past the Russian style church of St Peter and Paul, famous for its Glockenspiel bells that ring out hourly across the Havel. Both the church and the wooden houses at Nikolskoe were built by Friedrich Wilhelm III as a gift for his daughter Charlotte who became Tsarina of Russia in 1825. The historic **Blockhaus Nikolskoe** has views across to the Pfaueninsel. Another twenty minutes further on is **Wirtshaus Moorlake**, built in 1840 as a forester's lodge. From here the riverside path to the Krugshorn looks across to the Sacrower Heilandskirche Church in Potsdam on the opposite bank.

The stunning parkland of Schloss Glienicke is now in view. It was designed for the first owner by Lenné as a 'pleasure ground' and the estate was bought in 1823 by 21 year old Prince Carl of Prussia. He had fallen in love with Italy and hired Schinkel to help him create a Mediterranean landscape in Brandenburg. Several Arcadian follies were added; a teahouse, a rotunda, a mock cloister using material from a monastery in Venice and the original house was transformed into a small Italian style palace, guarded by

Glienicke Bridge which links Berlin and Potsdam

two golden lions. After a tour of the palace, visitors can relax in the **Café Lenné** or enjoy a fine meal at the **Goldener Greif**.

The Glienicke Bridge across the Havel was once the frontier between East and West but now simply links Potsdam with West Berlin. During the Cold War it was ironically named 'Brücke der Einheit' (Bridge of Unity) by the GDR and was the scene of dramatic spy exchanges. It is hard to imagine such political tension in these romantic surroundings. On the other side of the main road is the peaceful haven of Klein-Glienicke by the Griebnitzsee. During the years of division this area was a GDR enclave, bizarrely cut off from West Berlin land and water by the Wall. Along the pretty old cobbled streets are Swiss-style chalets which were originally part of the Prussian royal estate. There is a waterside restaurant and beer garden at the **Bürgershof** and when you can bear to leave, the 316 bus will take you back to Wannsee station.

Of course, there is much, much more to discover in Potsdam on the other side of the Glienicke Bridge. This beautiful city, capital of the Federal State of Brandenburg, played a central role in Prussia's history and is now a UNESCO World Heritage Site, best known for Frederick the Great's fabulous Schloss Sanssouci. Potsdam is only 10 minutes by train from Wannsee and merits a whole day's visit. It is easy to pick up a hop-on, hop-off Sightseeing Bus outside Potsdam station.

Liebe Leserin, lieber Leser,

wir freuen uns über Ihr Interesse an unserem Verlagsprogramm. Auch in Zukunft möchten wir Sie gern **kostenlos** über wichtige Themen informieren (per Post und E-Mail). Deshalb bitten wir Sie, diese Karte ausgefüllt an uns zurückzusenden.

Als Dank für Ihre Mitarbeit verlosen wir unter den Einsendern pro Monat ein Buch aus unserem Programm, das Ihren Interessen entspricht. (Der Rechtsweg ist ausgeschlossen)

Diese Karte habe ich folgendem Buch entnommen:

Ich interessiere mich für:

- ☐ Zeitgeschichte
- ☐ Geschichte
- ☐ Biografien
- ☐ Berlin
- ☐ Brandenburg
- ☐ Sachsen
- ☐ Belletristik
- ☐ Japan Edition
- ☐ Krimis
- ☐ Wissenschaft

Aufmerksam wurde ich auf das Buch durch:

☐

be.bra verlag
edition q / berlin edition

EXTRA-GEWINNCHANCE!
Besuchen Sie unsere Website
www.bebraverlag.de
und gewinnen Sie weitere attraktive Preise.

www.bebraverlag.de

Bitte als
Postkarte
freimachen

Antwort

**be.bra verlag GmbH
– Kundenbetreuung –
KulturBrauerei Haus S
Schönhauser Allee 37**

D-10435 Berlin

Tel.: 030 / 440 23 810   Fax: 030 / 440 23 819   post@bebraverlag.de

Absender

Name   Vorname

Straße

PLZ/Ort

E-Mail

Alter   Beruf

Zitadelle Spandau

Spandau

The furthest west and least-populated of the Berlin boroughs is Spandau, whose name is associated with its military prison, demolished in 1987 after the death of its last inmate, Hitler's Deputy, Rudolf Hess. Spandau was a town in its own right until 1920 and is older than Berlin. The Spandauers remain fiercely independent. They still talk about 'going to Berlin' as if it were a separate city and refer to the capital as 'Berlin near Spandau'. The old town is clustered around the imposing Rathaus and the 14th century St. Nikolai Kirche. The pretty streets of Hoher Steinweg and Möllentordamm have historic pubs like the **Spandauer Zollhaus**. But Spandau's real gem is the **Zitadelle**, one of the best-preserved Renaissance forts in Europe. Parts of it go back to the 13th century and the ancient **Juliusturm** has lovely views across the Havel.

Stage and Screen

Berlin is a cultural colossus. Some of the opera houses, concert halls, theatres and cinemas have legendary status and the range of entertainment is incredible. Since reunification the phoenix of the Roaring Twenties has risen from the ashes and Berlin is a world player on every kind of stage and screen. Events are listed in Zitty (www.zitty.de), Tip (www.tip-berlin.de) and Prinz (www.prinz.de) magazines. Tickets are available from Visit Berlin (tel: (030) 250 025; www.visitberlin.de) or directly through most venues.

Classical Music

Berlin's first golden era of culture started with Frederick the Great. He encouraged music to flourish at the Prussian court and his Kapelle became one of the most admired orchestras in Europe. An accomplished flautist, composer and ardent opera enthusiast, he was determined that Berlin should have an opera house to rival the splendid Semperoper in Dresden. He commissioned two opera stages, one in the Stadtschloss and a new royal court opera house on Unter den Linden. This was the time when Germany's rich musical life started to blossom and Berlin has never looked back. With three opera houses and seven symphony orchestras, including the world-famous Berlin Philharmonic, it is a paradise for fans of classical music.

Aurorasaal Schloss Köpenick

The Sunday afternoon concerts and recitals in this historic palace salon can be combined with a visit to Köpenick.
| 1 Schloßinsel, 12557 Berlin-Köpenick

Botanischer Garten

Outdoor concerts are staged here during the summer months. If it rains the proceedings are moved to the dramatic surroundings of the new glasshouse. In winter there are weekend palmhouse chamber music concerts.
| 5–10 Unter den Eichen, 12203 Berlin-Lichterfelde, www.bgbm.org

C Bechstein Centrum

Bechstein's flagship store in Stilwerk on Kantstraße stages occasional free concerts with world-class pianists.
| 17 Kantstraße, 10623 Berlin-Charlottenburg, www.bechstein-centren.de/berlin

Deutsche Oper

This company's history goes back to the Deutsches Opernhaus, opened in Charlottenburg in 1912. When the Nazis came to power Carl Ebert, the general manager, chose to emigrate and went on to co-found the Glyndebourne Opera Festival in England. The Deutsches Opernhaus was destroyed in an air raid and the new building, home to the Deutsche Oper and the Staatsballett Berlin, was opened in 1961. This is a monumental structure with clear lines and the auditorium follows the same rule of simplicity. Its outstanding acoustics and technical capabilities, combined with the high standard of the resident opera and ballet companies, attract top conductors and soloists.
| 35 Bismarckstraße, 10627 Berlin-Charlottenburg,
www.deutscheoperberlin.de

Haus des Rundfunks

Two of the original studios inside the oldest dedicated broadcasting building in the world are still used for live concerts. The imposing building opposite the Funkturm in Charlottenburg was opened in 1931 and has a tiled façade 150 metres long.
| 8–14 Masurenallee, 14057 Berlin-Charlottenburg, www.rbb-online.de

Hochschule für Musik Hanns Eisler

The gifted students at the East Berlin music academy behind the Gendarmenmarkt stage about 400 performances a year.
| 55 Charlottenstraße, 10117 Berlin-Mitte, www.hfm-berlin.de

Komische Oper

The third of Berlin's opera houses was home to various theatres between 1892 and 1945, including the renowned Metropoltheater devoted to Berlin revue and operetta. The exterior was destroyed during the last days of the war but the stage and auditorium survived. It was rebuilt in the mid-1960s with a new functional façade but the beautiful 19th century interior has been retained. The entertaining repertoire lives up to the description of 'opera as theatre'. Tickets are less expensive than for the two larger opera houses.
| 55–57 Behrenstraße, 10117 Berlin-Mitte, www.komische-oper-berlin.de

Inside the Konzerthaus, Mitte

Konzerthaus

Schinkel's early 19th century architectural jewel was destroyed in the bombing and finally restored in the 1980s. Originally built as a theatre under the name 'Schauspielhaus Berlin' it now contains two concert halls: a large hall for symphony concerts and a small one for chamber concerts. Both have been lavishly refurbished in a neo-classical style. The Beethoven Saal is especially impressive and the best spot for pre-concert or interval drinks.
| Gendarmenmarkt, 10117 Berlin-Mitte, www.konzerthaus.de

Orangerie, Schloss Charlottenburg

The 'Berliner Residenz' concerts are aimed at the tourist market and promise to 'take music lovers back in time – into Berlin's Baroque era'. There are concert packages that include dinner at the Orangerie, a tour of the Schloss and a Spree river cruise.
| 20 Spandauer Damm, 14059 Berlin-Charlottenburg, www.concerts-berlin.com

Philharmonie

The new home of the world-famous Berlin Philharmonic Orchestra caused great controversy when it first opened in 1963. Now Hans Scharoun's Philharmonie sits comfortably beside the massive tented roof of the Sony Center

Philharmonie, Tiergarten

on Potsdamer Platz. The acoustics of the terraced auditorium are legendary and there's not a bad seat in the house. Many Berliners have season tickets and in the days of Herbert von Karajan fans queued all night to get tickets. It pays to book well in advance for Berlin Philharmonic concerts; this orchestra is still at the top of its game and under Sir Simon Rattle the average age of players has gone down from 45 to 38. There are free Tuesday lunchtime concerts in the Philharmonie foyer from September to June.
| 1 Herbert-von-Karajan-Straße, 10785 Berlin-Tiergarten, www.berliner-philharmoniker.de

Radialsystem V

A 'new and creative space for the arts' hit Berlin in September 2006. Its building is a 19th century pumping station used by the Berlin waterworks until 1999. It has a unique urban location on the Spree at the meeting point of Mitte, Friedrichshain and Kreuzberg, 'radiating' new ideas in all directions. There are all kinds of concerts, galas, events and workshops and the venue comes into its own in the summer when you can watch the sunset from the terrace or enjoy Sunday brunch with live music. Classical music and dance feature extensively in the programme and the offerings are always innovative.
| 33 Holzmarktstraße, 10243 Berlin-Friedrichshain, www.radialsystem.de

Staatsoper, Mitte

Schloss Glienicke

There are wonderful afternoon recitals in this small 'palace' on the shores of the lake. Culture can be combined with a stroll through the parkland.
| 36 Königstraße, 14109 Berlin-Wannsee, www.schloss-glienicke.de

Schwartzsche Villa

This grand mansion built in 1895 for Berlin banker, Carl Schwartz, is now a cultural centre and the salon is used for classical recitals.
| 55 Grunewaldstraße, 12165 Berlin-Steglitz, www.schwartzsche-villa.de

Staatsoper

Frederick the Great wanted his Royal Opera House to be 'an enchanted castle'. Over its 250 year history the current 'Staatsoper' has been rebuilt several times but has never lost its magic. During the GDR years when it was state-run and non-elitist, performances of Borodin's Spartacus and Prokoviev's Romeo and Juliet captured the zeitgeist and played to packed houses. After reunification Daniel Barenboim was appointed General Music Director and the building is currently undergoing a total renovation. The Schiller Theater in Charlottenburg is serving as an alternative venue until 2013.
| 7 Unter den Linden, 10117 Berlin-Mitte, www.staatsoper-berlin.org

Stage and Screen

Universität der Künste

Bruch, Humperdinck and Hindemith taught at this West Berlin academy, part of the University of Arts. Recitals and concerts are held in its halls on Hardenbergstraße and Bundesallee.
| 43 Einsteinufer, 10587 Berlin-Charlottenburg, www.udk-berlin.de

Waldbühne

Built for the 1936 Olympics, Hitler's box once stood in the middle section of this 'Forest Theatre' and the surroundings were decorated with athletic statues. The Rolling Stones played here in 1965 and today the Waldbühne is still a great venue for top names, plus the traditional annual appearance of the Berlin Philharmonic. Early booking is essential for this concert.
| 1 Glockenturmstraße, 14053 Berlin-Charlottenburg, www.waldbuehne-berlin.de

Music in Churches

Several historic Berlin churches provide heavenly settings for classical music. Free organ recitals are held in the Marienkirche at 1.30pm on Thursdays and Fridays, in the Sophienkirche on Fridays at 4pm and in the Kaiser-Wilhelm-Gedächtnis-Kirche on Saturdays at 6pm. The Berliner Dom, Kaiser-Wilhelm-Gedächtnis-Kirche, Französiche Friedrichstadtkirche, Gethsemanekirche and Auenkirche are the main venues for choral, orchestral and chamber concerts. The largest of Berlin's inner-city churches, Schinkel's St Elisabeth-Kirche, lay in ruins for 40 years, but is now gradually being restored and provides an atmospheric space for classical concerts.

Auenkirche, 118 Wilhelmsaue, 10715 Berlin-Wilmersdorf
Berliner Dom, Am Lustgarten, 10178 Berlin-Mitte
Französiche Friedrichstadtkirche, 5 Gendarmenmarkt, 10117 Berlin-Mitte
Gethsemanekirche, 77 Stargarder Straße, 10437 Berlin-Prenzlauer Berg
Kaiser-Wilhelm-Gedächtnis-Kirche, Breitscheidplatz, 10789 Berlin-Charlottenburg
Marienkirche, 8 Karl-Liebknecht-Straße, 10178 Berlin-Mitte
Sophienkirche, 31 Große Hamburger Straße, 10115 Berlin-Mitte
St. Elisabeth-Kirche, 3 Invalidenstraße, 10789 Berlin- Mitte
www.travelsignposts.com/Germany/sightseeing/classical-music-berlin-church

Theater des Westens, Charlottenburg

Theatre

The Berlin stage enjoyed its most spectacular success in the 1920s when the Weimar government essentially ended all forms of censorship, creating fertile ground for theatre and cabaret. The political chaos and economic hardship that followed were troubled times which writers and cabaret artists exploited with spectacular success.

On the classical stage the Deutsches Theater under Max Reinhardt was one of the leading theatres of the world and it was here that Bertolt Brecht first came to work in Berlin in 1924. He went on to write groundbreaking plays and musicals until forced into exile. After the war Brecht returned to East Berlin to found the Berliner Ensemble. At the same time the West Berlin stage got back on its feet, helped by subsidies from the Federal Republic. In today's Berlin there is plenty on offer for English speakers, even in fringe theatres and cabaret clubs.

Admiralspalast

The Admiralspalast on Friedrichstraße was originally a bathhouse and club for Prussian soldiers. It was famous in the 1920s for its cabaret, operettas, spa and brothel. Hitler cleaned up the acts in the 1930s and installed a private box. The building was spared war damage and was used by Brecht

before it went into decline. Restored and reopened in 2006 (without the brothel) the programme includes theatre, comedy, concerts and musicals.
| 101 Friedrichstraße, 10117 Berlin-Mitte, www.admiralspalast.de

Amphitheater, Monbijoupark

In summer the Hexenkessel Hoftheater (Witches' Cauldron Court Theatre) transforms the banks of the Spree opposite Museumsinsel into a magical open-air theatre and in winter a puppet theatre stages Grimm fairytales. Everything is in German but it's worth taking a look.
| 3 Monbijoustraße, 10117 Berlin-Mitte, www.amphitheater-berlin.de

Bar jeder Vernunft

The art nouveau décor and mirrored walls create the perfect cabaret atmosphere in this 'Bar without any sense'. Shows are often in English.
| 24 Schaperstraße, 10719 Berlin-Wilmersdorf, www.bar-jeder-vernunft.de

Berliner Ensemble

This theatre has international standing and continues the tradition started in 1949 when Bertolt Brecht and his wife Helene Weigel set up a touring theatre group. Five years later it moved to its present building, originally the Neues Theater am Schiffbauerdamm. The neo-baroque interior makes it one of the most glamorous theatres in Germany. Non-German speakers need to look out for musicals such as Brecht's Threepenny Opera.
| 1 Bertolt-Brecht-Platz, 10117 Berlin-Mitte, www.berliner-ensemble.de

Bluemax Theater

The former Imax movie complex at Potsdamer Platz is now the permanent home of the Blue Man Group, a trio of mute performers in blue grease paint, latex bald caps, and black clothing. Their mixture of mime, comedy and tricks packs in the international crowds.
| 4 Marlene-Dietrich-Platz, 10785 Berlin-Tiergarten,
www.stage-entertainment.de/theater-events/bluemax-theater.html

Chamäleon

This great little variety theatre in the Hackesche Höfe started life as a ballroom. Its art nouveau interior has been lovingly restored and the atmosphere is intimate and authentic. Some amazing things happen on stage and there is a party atmosphere which often continues after the show.
| 40–41 Rosenthaler Straße, 10178 Berlin-Mitte, www.chamaeleonberlin.de

Deutsches Theater, Mitte

Deutsches Theater

The Deutsches Theater is an elegant classical building dating back to 1850. This is where the German public expect to see their top actors and directors and the most famous classical masterpieces. Productions sometimes have English surtitles.

| 13 Schumannstraße, 10117 Berlin-Mitte, www.deutschestheater.de

English Theatre Berlin

Founded in 1990 in an old Kreuzberg courtyard as 'Friends of Italian Opera', the actors are from English-speaking countries and the audience tends to be composed of native English speakers – there are over 100,000 of them living and working in Berlin.

| 40 Fidicinstraße, 10965 Berlin-Kreuzberg, www.etberlin.de

Friedrichstadtpalast

The Las Vegas style shows at the Friedrichstadtpalast are spectacular. The theatre was founded in 1867 and has starred big names like Dietrich, Gréco, Armstrong, Fitzgerald and Minelli. During February the prestigious GDR building becomes a main cinema for the Berlinale film festival.

| 107 Friedrichstraße, 10117 Berlin-Mitte, www.show-palace.eu

HAU 1, 2, 3

The original Hebbel-Theater am Ufer, named after German playwright Friedrich Hebbel, was built in 1907/08. Virtually undamaged during the war, it has a stunning mahogany auditorium and was designed by Oskar Kaufmann, one of the best known theatre architects of his time. HAU now has three venues in Kreuzberg – the Hebbel-Theater (HAU 1), Theater am Halleschen Ufer (HAU 2) and the small Theater am Ufer (HAU 3). They all specialise in experimental productions, many accessible to English speakers.
| HAU 1, 29 Stresemannstraße, 10963 Berlin-Kreuzberg
| HAU 2, 32 Hallesches Ufer, 10963 Berlin-Kreuzberg
| HAU 3, 10 Tempelhofer Ufer, 10963 Berlin-Kreuzberg
  www.hebbel-am-ufer.de

Kookaburra Comedy Club

Berlin's first dedicated comedy club in the heart of cool Mitte has English shows on Tuesdays evenings and late night Saturdays. They are catching on fast.
| 184 Schönhauser Allee, 10119 Berlin-Mitte, www.comedyclub.de

Maxim Gorki Theater

This historic theatre has a prime location just behind the Neue Wache on Unter den Linden and stages contemporary drama – all in German.
| 2 Am Festungsgraben, 10117 Berlin-Mitte, www.gorki.de

Renaissance Theater

Another beautiful Kaufmann theatre, but the classy dramatic repertoire is only of interest to German speakers. It also stages special shows and events in English.
| 100 Knesebeckstraße, 10623 Berlin-Charlottenburg, www.renaissance-theater.de

Schaubühne

The Schaubühne started as an independent theatre company and moved to the former Universum cinema on the Ku'damm in 1981, an iconic building designed by the Expressionist Jewish architect, Erich Mendelsohn, who emigrated to the USA in the 1930s. Wrapped around a street corner, it looks rather like a huge advertisement hoarding. The productions are equally unconventional and this is where West Berlin intellectual society hangs out. Once a month the production has English surtitles and there are sometimes other events in English.
| 153 Kurfürstendamm, 10709 Berlin-Wilmersdorf, www.schaubuehne.de

Schaubühne, Wilmersdorf

Schiller Theater

After the First World War the Schiller Theater served as the State Theatre of Berlin. In the late 1930s it was redesigned and during West Berlin days it staged 20th century masterpieces. The building is now a venue for concerts and musicals and until 2013 it is the temporary home of the Staatsoper.
| 110 Bismarckstraße, 10625 Berlin-Charlottenburg,
www.schiller-theater-berlin.de

Sophiensäle

This is one of Berlin's coolest theatre complexes, co-founded in the 1990s by Sasha Waltz and located in a series of historic craft workshops in the Sophienhöfe. The stage and dance productions are usually experimental and give opportunities for young artists.
| 18 Sophienstraße, 10178 Berlin-Mitte, www.sophiensaele.com

Theater am Potsdamer Platz

Glitzy musicals and ice shows are the standard fare here.
| 1 Marlene-Dietrich-Platz, 10785 Berlin-Tiergarten,
www.stage-entertainment.de/theater-events/theater-am-potsdamer-platz.html

Stage and Screen

Volksbühne, Mitte

Theater des Westens

The magnificent Gründerzeit building was opened in 1896 as part of Berlin's new west end and has presented world stars like Caruso, Dietrich and Callas. The accent is now on international hit musicals.
| 12 Kantstraße, 10623 Berlin-Charlottenburg,
www.stage-entertainment.de/theater-events/theater-des-westens.html

Tipi am Kanzleramt

The Tipi is a modern version of a traditional big top, perfect for variety and cabaret entertainment. In the good old days, beer gardens and cafés lined 'In den Zelten' (in the tents), a road in the Tiergarten so-called because in the 18th century refreshments were served in tents. The Tipi continues this tradition by serving dinner before the show.
| Große Querallee, 10557 Berlin-Tiergarten, www.tipi-am-kanzleramt.de

Volksbühne

Billed as 'Art for the People' the Volksbühne was designed by Kaufmann, opened in 1914 and rebuilt in the 1950s. It features political theatre and the Roter Salon and the Grüner Salon are popular music and clubbing venues.
| 227 Rosa-Luxemburg-Platz, 10178 Berlin-Mitte, www.volksbuehne-berlin.de

Wintergarten Theater

The Wintergarten's plush interior invites you to escape into a world of glamour and fun. The musicals, revues and shows have their roots in 19th century music hall tradition. You can dine before the show in the auditorium or in the restaurant.

| 96 Potsdamer Straße, 10785 Berlin-Tiergarten, www.wintergarten-berlin.de

Die Wühlmäuse

'The Voles' has been a big name in biting satire and comedy since 1960. Its new home is the former 'Naafi' club of the British Military on Theodor-Heuss-Platz. Performers include American singer-comedian, Gayle Tufts, from Massachusetts who has made Berlin her home and has her own take on classic cabaret combining German and English.

| 2–4 Pommernallee, 14052 Berlin-Charlottenburg, www.wuehlmaeuse.de

Cinema

Cinema is huge in Berlin – and it all started in the German capital when the Skladanowsky brothers demonstrated their 'Bioskop' in the Wintergarten in 1885. UFA (Universum Film AG) was founded in Berlin in 1917 and the German film industry soon became the largest in Europe.

In the 1920s UFA's success was partly due to inflation because film makers borrowed money which was vastly devalued by the time it had to be repaid. They also had some of the best film directors and the symbolism of German Expressionism worked brilliantly in silent films.

In 1933 the Nazis converted the Berlin film industry into a propaganda instrument. After the war the UFA fled to West Germany and its interests in the GDR were taken over by the state-owned DEFA, which continued to operate from the Babelsberg Studios near Potsdam. In 1951 West Berlin held the first Berlin Film Festival and the 'Berlinale' is now one of the most important dates in the film industry's calendar.

Berliners are great cinema-goers and the market is now mainly divided between the big multiplexes and smaller local or art-house cinemas. Several Berlin cinemas show films in their original language which are listed in film guides as OF. Films listed as OmU are shown in their original language, usually with German subtitles. Films shown in their original language with English subtitles are listed as OF mit engl. UT. In summer, the Freiluftkinos (open-air cinemas) also screen some films in English.

Cinemas showing films in English

Arsenal

Sony Center cinema showing an incredible range of films. Films in OF or OmU on Sundays.
| 2 Potsdamer Straße, 10785 Berlin-Tiergarten,
www.arsenal-berlin.de

Babylon Mitte

Expressionist building with organ used for silent movies. Sometimes shows OF films.
| 30 Rosa-Luxemburg-Straße, 10178 Berlin-Mitte, www.babylonberlin.de

Babylon Kreuzberg

Twin screen cinema showing good selection of films in English.
| 126 Dresdener Straße, 10999 Berlin-Kreuzberg,
www.yorck.de/kinos/detail/ 100008/Babylon

Central-Kino

Arthouse cinema in Haus Schwarzenberg, wide range of films in English.
| 39 Rosenthaler Straße, 10178 Berlin-Mitte, www.kino-central.de

CineStar at the Sony Center

Multiplex showing wide selection of OF films.
| 4 Potsdamer Straße, 10785 Berlin-Tiergarten,
www.cinestar.de/de/quickfinder/berlin-cinestar-original-im-sony-center

Eiszeit

Tiny Kreuzberg cinema showing non-mainstream films in English.
| 20 Zeughofstraße, 10997 Berlin-Kreuzberg,
www.eiszeitkino.de

Hackesche Höfe

Five-screen cinema. OmU films shown daily.
| 40/41 Rosenthaler Straße, 10178 Berlin-Mitte, www.hoefekino.de

Odeon

Traditional cinema in Schöneberg, all films in English.
| 116 Hauptstraße, 10827 Berlin-Schöneberg,
www.yorck.de/kinos/detail/ 100011/Odeon

Babylon Cinema, Mitte

UCI Kinowelt Colosseum

Historic building, latest releases in OF.
| 123 Schönhauser Allee, 10437 Berlin-Prenzlauer Berg, www.uci-kinowelt.de/Berlin_Colosseum

Open-Air Cinemas Freiluftkinos

From May to September Berlin has 19 open-air cinemas, some in parks where trees are hung with fairy lights and wooden shacks sell real food and drink instead of popcorn and coke. This is an essential Berlin summer evening experience. Films are often in the original version, especially in the Freiluftkino Kreuzberg. In the city centre you can enjoy the old courtyard setting of the Freiluftkino Mitte, join the joyful masses at the huge Freiluftkino Friedrichshain in the Volkspark or stretch out on a striped deckchair in the Sommerkino Kulturforum Potsdamer Platz. A full list with links to the individual cinemas is at www.berlin.de/kino.

Late Nightlife

By Johannes Jünemann

"Look at me! ... I am Babel, the monster among cities! We had a formidable army, now we command the most riotously wicked night life."

These words were written about Berlin by Klaus Mann in the 1920s when the old authorities of the German empire had crumbled. New nightlife was developing in theatres, bars and clubs around Friedrichstraße or in the artists' bars around Kurfürstendamm. At the Bahnhof Zoo people streamed into the cinemas that had just opened, while the area around Nollendorfplatz in Schöneberg saw the more eccentric versions of the activities going on in Friedrichstraße: gay bars, nude dance clubs, transvestite shows, easily available drugs. The city's nightlife was fast, exuberant, radical, and physically and mentally exhausting.

Fifty years on the political circumstances had changed dramatically, but the hedonistic nightlife remained. When David Bowie and Iggy Pop moved into 155 Hauptstraße in Berlin-Schöneberg in 1976, Berlin was a divided city. Monotony defined the image of the streets with run-down pre-war apartment buildings next to grey post-war apartment buildings. Bowie frequented the gay bars of Schöneberg and other artist hangouts, such as Anderes Ufer, Chez Romy Haag, Exil and Paris Bar. By the end of the 1970s West Berlin was isolated between superpowers engaged in a nuclear arms race; an apocalyptic spirit was palpable. Life was bleak and the city relied on subsidies from West Germany. Society's outsiders gathered here: those fleeing military service, artists, students, musicians, squatters, punks and oddballs. West Berlin came out with extreme forms of music such as the bands Einstürzende Neubauten, Malaria! or Die tödliche Doris. The genres Industrial, Neue Deutsche Welle (the German version of New Wave), Krautrock, Punk and electronic music developed here. Schöneberg and Kreuzberg were the centres of nightlife and the club SO36 opened its doors. In the East, subcultures could only form underground, since the 'United Socialist State' didn't approve of deviation from the norm.

The history of the 'Wende' (the turning point) in 1989 is also the history of the gradual establishment of Techno music as the main feature of the newly unified city's nightlife. In the course of the 1980s several genres of electronic music, Acid House, Chicago House and Detroit Techno, had started to catch on in both parts of the city. There is an obvious parallel between Detroit and Berlin; both were de-industrialised cities hard hit by economic depression but with large inner city spaces that seemed predestined for the emergence of new, creative cultural expression. After the Wall came down, it was East Berlin in particular that offered enormous vacant spaces after the old order had vanished. East and West Berlin's subcultures met in the inner city of former East Berlin. New bars, restaurants and clubs opened constantly and the authorities couldn't keep up with issuing new licences as no-one knew who owned the premises. Very often the establishments didn't stay long but moved on quickly elsewhere. The capital developed a lively nightlife where the locations and dates of parties were spread by word of mouth and Techno was the music of the hour.

Berlin's club landscape

In the 21st century Berlin's party culture continues to flourish. At weekends there are club nights around the clock – you can literally dance from Friday evening to Monday morning and the pursuit of escapism and exhaustion is still high on the agenda. The activities of the Techno subculture were the first to spread across the inner-city border – Berlin's nightlife was reunited long before its administrative authorities. Today Techno and electronic music remain the 'hard currency' of Berlin's nightlife. The city is regarded as the world capital of Techno and even though the pioneer days of the early 1990s may be over, many of the elements of that era's nightlife have been preserved. Clubs and bars continue to have a temporary quality, although several bigger clubs have established themselves for the long term in the city's nightlife landscape.

First and foremost is the **Berghain**. Located in a former thermal power plant this club enjoys a worldwide reputation for being the top club for Techno. Week after week it hosts the world's premier established and up-and-coming Techno and House DJs but it's the surroundings that work the magic. The interior is austere and raw and the industrial character of the power plant has been preserved. Photography is prohibited and the total absence of mirrors is meant to make people less self-conscious. The huge spaces, the powerful sound system and the regular crowd that expertly negotiates the vastness and the darkness in this environment combine to create an awe-inspiring experience for the first time visitor. The best time

Club der Visionäre, Treptow

in the Berghain is at 9am in the Panoramabar on the top floor. It's still dark inside and the clubber can't see what time of day it is outside. Then the blinds briefly open at the climax of the DJ's set and daylight fills the room. The crowd goes wild. This is a place for committed fans. If you're in Berlin for its famous techno nightlife, this is your premier address.

Berlin has a myriad of clubs for electronic music. One that has managed to establish a name is the **Watergate** club, on the bank of the river Spree, next to the Oberbaumbrücke in Kreuzberg. The large window panes offer stunning views across the water to the other shore and music is mostly House and Techno. The extended light installations on the upper dance floor ceiling function like an equaliser and in the early hours of the summer months clubbers can take a breather outside on a floating terrace while the bass is booming from inside.

In Berlin-Mitte the club **Weekend** on the 12th and 15th floor of the imposing Haus des Reisens attracts the top names and the roof terrace has magnificent views of Berlin. There's no better place to enjoy a music-accompanied sunrise over the city, from outside on early summer mornings when the roof is open or from inside in colder weather. The iconic **Tresor** moved to a new venue inside a former thermal power plant at Köpenicker Straße in Berlin-Mitte in 2007. The interior is still reminiscent of its legendary former

Late Nightlife

location with intricate light installations and industrial flair and still often hosts old Detroit Techno heroes. These clubs usually have a less strict door policy than the Berghain, but still there's no guarantee of entry.

Other notable clubs specializing in electronic music are the **Tape** near the Hauptbahnhof in Moabit, the **Maria** at Ostbahnhof, the **Horst** near Hallesches Tor, which frequently indulges in British dance music, as does the **About Blank** in Friedrichshain and the run-down **Golden Gate** near Jannowitzbrücke in Mitte.

During the summer months many clubs have open-air sections, whilst some clubs are exclusively designed for the summer season such as the **Club der Visionäre**, on a house-boat on the Landwehrkanal near Schlesisches Tor. After the open-air club **Bar 25** finally had to leave its premises on the banks of the Spree in 2010, its successor **Kater Holzig** opened the following summer in a former soap factory across the river. Clubbers continue where they left off a year earlier, dancing in this inner-city oasis at parties that stretch into the following week – provided they make it past the strict door policy.

Since Berlin's club landscape is so lively and spontaneous, it's always best to find out where the parties are taking place and which clubs have just opened on the internet or the weekly magazines. Good websites are **www.residentadvisor.com** and **www.berlin.unlike.net**. The English-speaking city magazine **Exberliner** and the two major German ones **Zitty** and **Tip** have all the information on events for a particular weekend.

Concert venues

Of course, Berlin's musical diversity consists of more genres than electronic music. For Indiepop and Indie Rock concerts the clubs **Lido** and **Magnet** in Kreuzberg and **Astra Kulturhaus** in Friedrichshain are the top addresses in the city. These medium-sized venues usually host current Indiebands from the English-speaking world, Scandinavia and Germany. The **Festsaal Kreuzberg** serves up a similar selection. Kreuzberg's **SO36** started out as a Punk venue and still hosts mainly Punk and Hardcore bands. Its musical range has widened though, so that even electronic clubnights and Turkish and Arabic music have found a home here. Other places for occasional Indie concerts are **Roter Salon** and **Grüner Salon** in Mitte. The **C-Club** offers national and international Indie Rock, Electronica, Post-Rock and Hip Hop acts. Formerly called Columbia Club this venue near Tempelhof Airport was originally a cinema built for American soldiers. The

Arena, Treptow

C-Halle nearby is the bigger brother of this venue. British and American bands play at **Huxleys Neue Welt** in Neukölln and **Postbahnhof** in Friedrichshain and **Arena** in Treptow are also worth checking out as concert venues – both these places stage electronic music festivals as well. In the summer international big names usually play the huge **Olympiastadion** or the **Waldbühne** or its East-Berlin equivalent **Kindl-Bühne** at the park Wuhlheide. Another venue for the bigger bands is the **Tempodrom**. Like many other European cities, Berlin has been blessed with an O_2-**Arena**, built right by the Spree opposite the East Side Gallery. In the Berlin version you can follow the city's hockey and basketball clubs and see the bigger international music acts throughout the year.

Musical acts of a more avant-garde variety perform at the **Volksbühne**, a theatre in Mitte which makes a good concert venue and has a fantastic selection of musical acts. Among a host of small clubs **West Germany** is worth noting. This features underground, international and German acts and is situated behind a plain steel door on Skalitzer Straße at Kottbusser Tor with no sign of any kind to advertise the club. **Antje Øklesund** is another slightly hidden concert venue where smaller local and international bands perform. To reach it you have to cross an industrial yard at Rigaer Straße, Friedrichshain.

Kaffee Burger, Mitte

By comparison, Berlin's numerous Jazz clubs come with a slightly more laid-back ambience. Former West Berlin is a good area for this type of music with Mitte having caught up in recent years. The venerable **A-Trane** and **Quasimodo** in Charlottenburg, the **Badenscher Hofclub** in Wilmersdorf and Mitte Jazz bars **Schlot** and **b-flat** are all popular with Jazz fans. But even Neukölln has something on offer, such as the fairly recent **Fincan** which features Jazz and World Music concerts at the weekends.

The list of small bars and informal concert venues that host lesser known local and international musical artists every night is endless. They can be found in every district of the inner city. Just to give a few examples there are **Intersoup** and **Duncker** in Prenzlauer Berg, the **Junction Bar** in Kreuzberg, the **Kaffee Burger** and **Schokoladen** in Mitte and the **Laika** in Neukölln. Again it's advisable to find out on the internet, from your hotel or in the city magazines which places are nearby.

Nightlife districts

Since 1990 young people, students and artists have been drawn to the East-Berlin inner city districts such as Mitte, Friedrichshain and Prenzlauer Berg where lively nightlife quarters have developed. But this trend has now started

Astra Kulturhaus, Friedrichshain

to turn around. West Berlin's forgotten districts are being rediscovered and the scene is increasingly moving into Neukölln, Schöneberg and Wedding as well.

There is a particularly lively area on both sides of the Oberbaumbrücke in Friedrichshain and Kreuzberg. On the Friedrichshain side the bars on Simon-Dach-Straße and its side streets are packed every night. Tourists mix with Berliners in places with names like **Dachkammer, Astro-Bar** and **Raumklang** and the party atmosphere keeps going till the small hours. Further south the **RAW-area** is located in what used to be the maintenance site for the East German railway company. These days the repair workshops house cultural facilities such as bars, clubs and venues that use the existing industrial infrastructure and turn it into something unique. As with many of these Berlin sites its future is under dispute. Plans for turning it into a residential area have surfaced, but as long as they don't take effect, the RAW-area remains a fantastic nightlife spot. Other recommendations are **MIKZ** for electronic music, the laid-back, partly open-air club **Rosi's** and **Cassiopeia, Astra Kulturhaus** and the **Suicide Circus**.

On the other side of the Oberbaumbrücke lies the pulsating area around Schlesisches Tor in Kreuzberg. The clubs **Watergate, Lido, Magnet, Lux** and **Club der Visionäre** among others are located here. On summer nights

SO36, Kreuzberg

the streets around Schlesisches Tor are teeming with people and there are masses of bars. **Madame Claude** has an upside-down interior and **Konrad Tönz** is a pleasant laid-back place where you can take it easy before or after hitting the clubs. The area around Oranienstraße and Kottbusser Tor has been living off its multicultural and leftist reputation since the 1980s. Along Oranienstraße there are lots of bars and pubs where you can spend a long night out, even if you don't feel like clubbing. For serious beer drinking the pub **Franken** is recommended, or the slightly rougher **Trinkteufel**. The established clubs **SO36**, **West Germany** and **Festsaal Kreuzberg** are located in this area but for a more upmarket atmosphere, the district around Bergmannstraße in Kreuzberg 61 has plenty of bars and pubs where you can easily spend a whole night exploring the scene. A new distinct nightlife area has developed in the bar/club scene along Skalitzer Straße. Beginning at Kottbusser Tor and moving eastwards new, mostly small clubs have been established such as **Monarch**, **Paloma Bar**, **Bar 7000**, **Farbfernseher** and **Kleine Reise**. These places share a fine selection of electronic music acts and a great atmosphere on busy weekend nights.

In Prenzlauer Berg the area around Eberswalder Straße station is probably the most vibrant in the district. To the south is the **KulturBrauerei**, a former brewery. Compared to the converted site of the RAW-area this one is

Schokoladen, Mitte

renovated and generally more chic. At the southern end of Schönhauser Allee lies the little nightlife triangle of **8mm Bar**, **White Trash Fast Food** and the venue **Pfefferberg**. The **8mm Bar** is a pleasantly loud, uninhibited place with a nice interior and mostly rock music. At weekends it's packed with an international crowd. The venue/restaurant **White Trash Fast Food** has gained a reputation over the years for its nutritious burgers and at times gruff service, both of which are being increasingly appreciated by the over 40s. The venue's interior is a wild but fitting mixture of Chinese restaurant and Western saloon bar. To the south-west of Eberswalder Straße station stretches the Kastanienallee where there is a string of bars and restaurants. A visit to the **Prater Biergarten** on a warm summer evening is a must. The southern end of Kastanienallee merges into Weinbergsweg which leads to Rosenthaler Platz, another nightlife quarter of its own.

We are now in Mitte where **Schokoladen** and **Tacheles** are both cultural oases, threatened with closure year after year since they inhabit expensive coveted spaces right in the city centre. The cosy Schokoladen often hosts small Indie concerts by international artists. Tacheles is a former Jewish department store that was heavily damaged during the Second World War and has been squatted by an art collective since 1990. Since 2010 it has been subject to repeated evictions and parts of it have been sold off and cleared.

Frannz Club, KulturBrauerei, Prenzlauer Berg

The remaining artists are doing their best to keep things going, but the future of this magical place remains unclear. Just north of Rosenthaler Platz is **ZMF** in the second courtyard of a Brunnenstraße building. This is a small but likably unpretentious club for electronic music. A few metres down Rosenthaler Straße is **Delicious Doughnuts**, a similar place that works well after a party. Somewhat more commercialized is the area around Hackescher Markt which also has a lively nightlife in the bars of Hackesche Höfe. There are concerts and Indie club nights at **Levee** and **Roter** and **Grüner Salon** in this area. If it's a super sleek nightclub you're looking for, then **Bar Tausend** behind the iron door under the railway bridge on Schiffbauerdamm or **Cookies** on Friedrichstraße will fit the bill. These are places to see and to be seen in.

The nightlife district around Weserstraße in Northern Neukölln has emerged fairly recently. It boasts small, often eccentric bars and bigger, established ones that have only existed for a couple of years. It has a reputation as an artists' quarter and has seen a massive influx of young people in recent times. Recommendations for this area are the bar **Ä**, which is frequented by a relatively young, very international crowd. A somewhat more down to earth pub of similar size is the **Freies Neukölln**. The ever-changing smaller bars and venues are best explored spontaneously when you're

Grüner Salon in der Volksbühne, Mitte

there. A similar development can be detected in parts of Wedding, where the former town swimming pool (Stadtbad) has been turned into a gallery and club whose witty name **Stattbad Wedding**, means 'instead of a pool'.

Berlin has a vast choice of nightlife venues and every district of the city has its own unique infrastructure. Regulations, if they exist at all, are liberal. Most bars are open until the last customer wants to go home which means that the binge-drinking and obligatory partying present in other European capitals is pleasantly absent. Prices for drinks and entrances are held at a reasonable level, as it's a poor city with a high unemployment level. Yet there remains a lot of space for creativity and new things. Berlin has become a central meeting place for young people around the world who are seeking the kind of freedom that their wealthier but over-regimented home cities lack. It is still a city of excess, hedonism and escapism. The nightlife scene has so much to offer that everyone can decide for themselves what they want to savour and to what extent – and nobody takes the slightest notice or cares. It is this freedom that makes Berlin's nightlife so special.

Café Society

Like everything else in the German capital, food and drink have been liberated from all constraints. The local laws have even been relaxed to allow designated smoking areas. Food snobbery hardly exists and the service is friendly and relaxed nearly everywhere, although sometimes the Berlin sardonic humour is part of the deal. Twelve coveted Michelin stars have been awarded to top Berlin restaurants but it's accepted that they are likely to be a bit younger, fresher and different. In many ways Berlin cuisine is a reflection of the social situation of the city – a melting pot of traditions and flavours from all over the world.

Berlin Specialities

Since President Kennedy got his German grammar wrong, everyone knows that an edible 'Berliner' is the local word for a doughnut. Other Berlin specific terms are 'Schrippe' for a bread roll and 'Stulle' for a slice of bread. Top of the Berlin fast-food list is the Currywurst, a sausage covered in tomato sauce with curry spice sprinkled on top. There are Currywurst stands all over the city, some with legendary status. Another favourite snack is a 'Boulette', a cross between a meatball and a hamburger or a Döner Kebab, the Turkish fast-food invented in Kreuzberg. Traditional 'Old Berlin' restaurant specialities are warming in winter, especially the soups. Erbsensuppe (pea), Linsensuppe (lentil) and Gulaschsuppe all make a filling meal. 'Eisbein' is knuckle of pork and 'Königsberger Klopse' a Prussian dish of meatballs in creamy sauce. Beer is an essential part of the Berlin drinking culture with Berliner Pilsner top of the list. A popular summer drink is 'Berliner Weiße', beer with a shot of red or green fruit juice served in a punch glass and drunk through a straw.

Café culture

Berliners spend hours hanging out in their local café or bar. They love to go out for breakfast or brunch and many places have a different set lunch for each day of the week. The tradition of afternoon coffee and cakes still lingers, but has largely been usurped by baristas and brownies in the city centre. Here food and drink are served all day long and until later in the evening than in most other European cities. There never seems to be any pressure to leave – just make sure you can pay in cash as credit cards are not always accepted. Tipping used to be just a case of 'rounding up' but if the service is good at least 10% is expected. There are lively restaurants, cafés and bars almost everywhere and tables fill the wide pavements – with heaters and blankets on chairs if needed. In winter heavy felt curtains just inside the restaurant door are a wonderful way of locking in the warmth.

This list of places to eat and drink is a selection of tried and tested personal recommendations. The different neighbourhoods are described in 'Small Worlds'. To make a telephone booking the prefix is 004930 from abroad or a mobile/cell phone.

Mitte

Alt-Berliner Kaffeestuben
1 Fürstenberger Straße
☎ 449 51 51
Traditional

Anna Koschke
11 Krausnickstraße
☎ 283 55 38
Home-made dishes

Altes Europa
11 Gipsstraße
☎ 28 09 38 40
Berlin atmosphere

Arema
30 Birkenstraße
☎ 018 57 36
Good value in Moabit

Bandol sur mer
167 Torstraße
☎ 67 30 20
French gem, Brad Pitt loved it

Barcomi's Deli
21 Sophienstraße
☎ 28 50 83 63
Good bagels

Beth Café
60 Tucholskystraße
☎ 281 31 35
Warm ambience

Bierbrunnen
3 Behmstraße
☎ 493 95 03
Pub in Wedding supports Hertha BSC Berlin

Bocca di Bacco
167 Friedrichstraße
☎ 20 67 28 28
Stylish, Italian, expensive

Bonfini
3 Memhardstraße
☎ 24 72 66 70
Good value Italian home cooking

Borchhardt
47 Französische Straße
☎ 188 62 62
Berlin classic, marble columns

BöseBubenBar
18 Marienstraße
☎ 27 59 69 09
Cool place for brunch

Bötzow-Privat
113 Linienstraße
☎ 28 09 53 90
Berlin atmosphere

Brauhaus Georgbräu
4 Spreeufer, Nikolaiviertel
☎ 242 42 44
Beer by the Spree

Brechts
6 Schiffbauerdamm
☎ 28 59 85 85
Postmodern Austrian

Café Bravo
69 Auguststraße
☎ 23 45 77 77
Arty

Café Cinema
39 Rosenthaler Straße
☎ 280 64 15
Candles on tables,
good value

Café Neu
32 Oranienburger Straße
☎ 66 40 84 27
Courtyard cuisine

Clärchens Ballhaus
24 Auguststraße
☎ 282 92 95
Pre-war haunt, all ages,
live music

Cookies Cream
55 Behrenstraße
☎ 27 49 29 40
Stylish, vegetarian

Buchhandlung
32 Tucholskystraße
☎ 40 04 29 34
Student café-bar

Deckshaus
1z Märkisches Ufer
☎ 21 79 14 04
Café on historic boat

Dicker Engel
44 Birkenstraße
☎ 39 80 90 03
Old pub in Moabit

***Die Ständige
Vertretung***
8 Schiffbauerdamm
☎ 282 39 65
Lively, cult political pub/
restaurant

Eschenbräu
67 Triftstraße
☎ 462 68 37
Pub/brewery in Wedding

Ganymed Brasserie
5 Schiffbauerdamm
☎ 282 39 65
French flair, GDR history

***Good Time
Thai Restaurant***
11 Hausvogteiplatz
☎ 28 04 60 15
Best Asian in Mitte

Grill Royal
105b Friedrichstraße
☎ 28 87 92 88
Beloved by the glitterati,
book first

Honigmond
28 Borsigstraße
☎ 284 45 50
GDR dissidents met here

Kellerrestaurant
125 Chausseestraße
☎ 282 38 43
Authentic food in cellar of
Brecht's house, book first

Keyser Soze
33 Tucholskystraße
☎ 28 59 94 89
Friendly café/bar

Kunstfabrik Schlot
18 Chausseestraße
☎ 448 21 60

La Bonne Franquette
110 Chausseestraße
☎ 99 40 53 63
Bistro charm

Mädchen Italiener
12 Alte Schönhauser Straße
☎ 40 04 17 87
Central, relaxed

Mein Haus am See
197 Brunnenstraße
☎ 23 88 35 61
Open 24 hours for chilling

Mittendrin
19 Sophienstraße
☎ 28 49 77 40
'In the thick of things',
set lunch

Monsieur Vong
46 Alte Schönhauser Straße
☎ 99 29 69 24
Packed with locals,
fairly priced Asian food

Nola's am Weinberg
9 Veteranenstraße
☎ 440 40 77
Swiss, large terrace

Opernpalais
7 Unter den Linden
☎ 28 39 18 86
Prime location,
lovely terrace

Oxymoron
40 Rosenthaler Straße
☎ 28 39 18 86
Café, restaurant, bar, club

Paris Moskau
141 Alt-Moabit
☎ 394 20 81
19th century charm

Pro Macchina da Caffe
173 Ackerstraße
☎ 40 50 16 50
Perfect espresso

Reinstoff
26c Schlegelstraße
☎ 30 88 12 14
Michelin star, great setting and design

Remake Berlin
32 Große Hamburger Str.
☎ 20 05 41 02
Nouvelle cuisine

Restaurant Hackescher Hof
40 Rosenthaler Straße
☎ 283 52 93
Central brasserie

Restaurant Ruz
63 Auguststraße
☎ 28 09 77 88
Tapas, good wine

Restaurant Simon
53 Auguststraße
☎ 27 89 03 00
Historic cellar, fresh Italian food

Schrader's
16b Malplaquetstr.
☎ 45 08 26 63
Café-bar in Wedding

Schwarze Pumpe
76 Choriner Straße
☎ 449 69 39
GDR nostalgia

Schwarzwaldstuben
48 Tucholskystraße
☎ 28 09 80 84
Lively, South German

Sophien 11
11 Sophienstraße
☎ 283 21 36
Traditional, pretty garden

Sophieneck
37 Große Hamburger Str.
☎ 283 40 65
Historic pub-restaurant

Strandbad Mitte
16 Kleine Hamburger Str.
☎ 24 62 89 63
Scene café-bar

Theodor Tucher
6a Pariser Platz
☎ 22 48 94 63
Fine café by the Gate

Tucholsky Restauration
189 Torstraße
☎ 281 73 49

VAU Restaurant
54–55 Jägerstraße
☎ 202 97 30
Exclusive, stylish, top chef

Vox Restaurant, Grand Hyatt Hotel
2 Marlene-Dietrich-Platz
☎ 25 53 17 72
German tapas in the 'mesa' room

Weihenstephaner
5 Neue Promenade
☎ 84 71 07 60
Vaulted cellars, Bavarian

Weltempfänger
27 Anklamer Straße
☎ 44 35 69 81
Café by day, bar by night

You're Welcome
15 Große Hamburger Str.
☎ 282 76 57
Salads and soups

Zagreus Projekt
9a Brunnenstraße
☎ 28 09 56 40
Gallery owner/chef Krauss concocts meals for exhibitions.
Reservations only

Zum Nussbaum
3 Am Nussbaum
Nikolaiviertel
☎ 242 30 95
Small tavern, low ceilings

Zur letzten Instanz
14 Waisenstraße
☎ 242 55 28
Napoleon and Beethoven ate here

Strandbad Mitte, Prenzlauer Berg.

Prenzlauer Berg

Alt-Wien
22 Hufelandstraße
☎ 70 12 96 10
Austrian cuisine

An einem Sonntag im August
103 Kastanienallee
☎ 44 05 12 28
Apocalypse chic

Anna Blume
83 Kollwitzstraße
☎ 44 04 86 41
Coffee and flowers

Ars Vini
27 Sredzkistraße
☎ 54 71 41 82
Hip fondue restaurant

Café Morgenrot
85 Kastanienallee
☎ 44 31 78 44
Wooden tables, vegetarian

Café Chagall
2 Kollwitzstraße
☎ 441 58 81
Bohemian café-bar

Cenacolo
23 Sredzkistraße
☎ 44 04 47 43
Mediterranean feel

Chez Maurice
39 Bötzowstraße
☎ 425 05 06
French cuisine

Gugelhof
59 Kollwitzstraße
☎ 442 92 29
Alsace cuisine

I Due Forni
(one of three branches)
12 Schönhauser Allee
☎ 44 01 73 33
Punk pizza

Kaffeeraum
25 Bötzowstraße
☎ 50 56 24 10
Friendly, design interior

Kauf dich glücklich
44 Oderberger Straße
☎ 50 15 47 91

One of the oldest beer gardens, Prater Garten, Prenzlauer Berg

Konnopke's Imbiß
44b Schönhauser Allee
☎ 442 77 65
Currywurst since 1930

Lafil
33 Wörther Straße
☎ 28 59 90 26
Tapas weekend brunch

Metzer Eck
33 Metzer Straße
☎ 442 76 56
Old family pub

November
15 Husemannstraße
☎ 442 84 25
Easy-going local favourite

Pasternak
22 Knaackstraße
☎ 441 33 99
Russian brunch

Prater Garten
7 Kastanienallee
☎ 448 56 88
Huge historic beer garden

Restauration 1900
1 Husemannstraße
☎ 442 24 94
Nostalgic, stylish

Rote Lotte
38 Oderberger Straße
☎ 318 68 68

Sasaya
50 Lychener Straße
☎ 44 71 77 21
Top Sushi

Sowohlalsauch
88 Kollwitzstraße
☎ 442 93 11

The Bird
5 Am Falkplatz
☎ 51 05 32 83
Great steakhouse,
book first

Weinschenke Weinstein
33 Lychener Straße
☎ 441 18 42

Werkstatt der Suesse
25 Husemannstraße
☎ 259 01 57
Cake maker in action
on Saturdays

Freischwimmer, Kreuzberg

Wohnzimmer
6 Lettestraße
☎ 445 54 58
Old sofas, cool nightlife

Kreuzberg

Altes Zollhaus
30 Carl-Herz-Ufer
☎ 692 33 00
Historic, fine dining

Ankerklause
104 Kottbusser Damm
☎ 693 56 49
Juke box, parties, brunch

Baraka
6 Lausitzer Platz
☎ 612 63 30

Bar Centrale
82 Yorkstraße
☎ 786 29 89

Brachvogel
34 Carl-Herz-Ufer
☎ 693 04 32

Burgermeister
8 Oberbaumstraße
☎ 22 43 64 93
Late night burgers
under railway arches

Café Stresemann
90 Stresemannstraße
☎ 261 17 60
Historic setting

Curry 36
36 Mehringdamm
☎ 251 73 68
Best currywurst in West
Berlin, open all hours

3 Schwestern
2 Mariannenplatz
☎ 600 31 86 00
Good atmosphere any time

edelweiss
1–3 Görlitzer Straße
☎ 610 748 58

Felix Austria
26 Bergmannstraße
☎ 694 44 40
Great Schnitzel

Café Society

Freischwimmer
2a Vor dem Schlesischen Tor
☎ 61 07 43 09
Weeping willows

Fuchsbau
95 Planufer
☎ 691 75 95

G wie Gulasch
1 Chamissoplatz
☎ 21 46 66 09
Corner pub,
good soups

Golgatha
40–64 Dudenstraße
☎ 785 24 53

Hasir
10 Adalbertstraße
☎ 614 23 73
One of six branches

Hegeles Teufelsküche
22 Nostitzstraße
☎ 61 65 11 00
Good value,
relaxed atmosphere

Henne
25 Leuschnerdamm
☎ 614 77 30
Historic, fried chicken,
book first

Horvàth
44a Paul-Lincke-Ufer
☎ 61 28 99 92
Fine dining

Il Casolare Trattoria
30 Grimmstraße
☎ 69 50 66 10
Noisy pizza and pasta

Katerschmaus
23 Michaelkirchstraße
☎ 51 05 21 34
Shabby-chic, top floor
of old soap factory

Kimchi Princess
36 Skalitzer Straße
☎ 0163 458 02 03

King of Falafel
9 Graefestraße
☎ 74 07 36 66
Top falafel and halloumi

Knofi
98 Bergmannstraße
☎ 694 58 07
Colourful delicatessen
and restaurant

La Buvette
59 Forsterstraße
☎ 50 36 18 87
Charming bistro,
retro atmosphere

Mercan
10 Wiener Straße
☎ 61 28 58 41
Turkish for locals

*Mustafa's
Gemüse Kebab*
32 Mehringdamm
Vegetarian fast food

Osteria 1
71 Kreuzbergstraße
☎ 786 91 62
Established Italian

Riehmers Hofgarten
83 Yorckstraße
☎ 78 09 88 00

Sale e Tabbachi
25 Rudi-Dutschke-Straße
☎ 252 11 55
Historic building near
Checkpoint Charlie

Senti
17a Glogauer Straße
☎ 740 73 09
Lively tapas bar

Stadtklause
35 Bernburger Straße
☎ 93 51 05 63 81
Unique pre-war Berlin
experience behind
Potsdamer Platz,
best lunchtime

*Weltrestaurant
Markthalle*
34 Pücklerstraße
☎ 617 55 02
Authentic pub by old
market hall

*Wirtshaus
Max und Moritz*
162 Oranienstraße
☎ 69 51 59 11
Berlin atmosphere,
evenings only

Wirtshaus Max und Moritz, Kreuzberg

Yorckschlösschen
15 Yorckstraße
☎ 215 80 70

■ Friedrichshain

Henselmann Bistro
75 Karl-Marx-Allee
☎ 42 08 72 90
Good food, genuine service

Café Alberts
35 Karl-Marx-Allee
☎ 24 72 72 50
Large lively café-bar

Café Datscha
1 Gabriel-Max-Straße
☎ 70 08 67 35
Second Russian home,
good Sunday brunch

Café Moskau
34 Karl-Marx-Allee
☎ 200 75 60

Café Schönbrunn
im Volkspark Friedrichshain
☎ 42 02 81 91
70s GDR pavilion in park
by lake

Café Sibylle
72 Karl-Marx-Allee
☎ 29 35 22 03
Café with museum

Cupcake
12 Krossener Straße
☎ 25 76 86 87
Trendy cakes

Il Ritrovo
29 Wühlischstraße
☎ 29 36 41 30
Hectic, quirky, good pizza

Schneeweiß
16 Simplonstraße
☎ 904 97 04
Snow-white décor, fine food

Volckswirtschaft
17 Krossener Straße
☎ 69 20 68 61
Good organic food

■ Charlottenburg/Wilmersdorf

A-Trane
1 Bleibtreustraße
☎ 313 25 50

Café Society

Dollinger, Charlottenburg

Café Bleibtreu
45 Bleibtreustraße
☎ 881 47 56
Unpretentious, good value

Café Brel
1 Savignyplatz
☎ 31 80 00 20
Perfect bistro

Café im Literaturhaus
23 Fasanenstraße
☎ 882 54 14
Beautiful surroundings

Café Kranzler
18 Kurfürstendamm
☎ 887 18 39 25

Café Richter
22 Giesebrechtstraße
☎ 324 37 22
1970s retro,
 loved by locals

Dicke Wirtin
9 Carmerstraße
☎ 312 49 52
Old Berlin pub with character

Dollinger
1 Stuttgarter Platz
☎ 323 87 83
In string of cafés on friendly square

Engelbecken
31 Witzlebenstraße
☎ 615 28 10
By pretty lake

Florian
52 Grolmanstraße
☎ 313 91 84
Charming owners,
great food

Heising
32 Rankestraße
☎ 213 39 52
Aristocratic dining room

Il Calice
4 Walter-Benjamin-Platz
☎ 324 23 08
Italian, good wine list

*Kempinski Eck
(Reinhards im
Kempinski)*
27 Kurfürstendamm
☎ 88 43 40

Reinhard's im Kempinski, Charlottenburg

Kurpfalz Weinstuben
93 Wilmersdorfer Straße
☎ 883 66 64
Historic interior

Manstein
32 Witzlebenstraße
☎ 30 11 25 21

Marjellchen
9 Mommsenstraße
☎ 883 26 76
East Prussian menu,
good service

Meineke X
10 Meineke Straße
☎ 882 31 58

Mommseneck
45 Mommsenstraße
☎ 324 25 80

mr hai & Friends
1 Savignyplatz
☎ 37 59 12 00
Vietnamese, great value

Paris Bar
152 Kantstraße
☎ 313 80 52
A legend, fine food

Restaurant Lietzenburg
61 Schloßstraße
☎ 341 26 78
Pretty garden

Schwarzes Café
148 Kantstraße
☎ 313 80 38
Forever-young crowd,
open 24 hours

Silber Antik Café
2 Walter-Benjamin-Platz
☎ 310 166 16

Stattcafé
31 Suarezstraße
☎ 36 44 50 30
Local charm

Stella Alpina
4 Suarezstraße
☎ 322 28 05
Established,
delicious Italian

Weyers Restaurant
16 Pariser Straße
☎ 881 93 78
Insider tip near Ku'damm

Café Society

Zillemarkt
48 Bleibtreustraße
☎ 881 70 40
Old Berlin charm

Zwiebelfisch
5 Savignyplatz
☎ 312 73 63
Ageing hippies,
amateur philosophers

■ Schöneberg

Amrit
40 Winterfeldtstraße
☎ 21 01 46 40

Berio
7 Maaßenstraße
☎ 216 19 46

Café Bilderbuch
28 Akazienstraße
☎ 78 70 60 57
Charming café

Café Einstein
58 Kurfürstenstraße
☎ 263 91 90
Beautiful intelligentsia

Dolce Pizza
6 Maaßenstraße
☎ 20 05 15 85

Double Eye
22 Akazienstraße
☎ 0179-456 69 60

*Duke Restaurant,
Ellington Hotel*
50–55 Nürnberger Str.
☎ 68 31 540 00
Fine food and jazz

Gaststätte Gottlob
17 Akazienstraße
☎ 78 70 80 95
Well-loved local haunt

Habibi
24 Goltzstraße
☎ 215 33 32

Impala
5 Maaßenstraße
☎ 21 91 38 12

Joseph Roth Diele
75 Potsdamer Straße
☎ 26 36 98 84
1920s atmosphere,
dedicated to Jewish writer,
good value lunch

Literatur Hotel
68 Fregestraße
☎ 859 09 60

Mister Hu
39 Goltzstraße
☎ 217 21 11

Osteria Ribaltone
54 Motzstraße
☎ 214 36 55
Best food on
Viktoria-Luise-Platz

Renger Patzsch
54 Wartburgstraße
☎ 784 20 59
Alsace cuisine,
good atmosphere

Romantica Bar Central
7a Akazienstraße
☎ 784 55 18
Warm Berlin ambience

TeeTeaThe
2 Goltzstraße
☎ 21 75 22 40

Toronto
17 Crellestraße
☎ 781 92 30
Good location, friendly local

■ Tiergarten/ Potsdamer Platz

Café am Neuen See
2 Lichtensteinallee
☎ 254 49 30
Sunny weekends in the
Tiergarten

Capt'n Schillow
113 Straße des 17. Juni
☎ 315 50 15
Restaurant on boat,
near antique market

Käfer's Dachgarten
Reichstag
☎ 22 62 99 00
Great views, fine food

Schleusenkrug
1 Müller-Breslau-Straße
☎ 313 99 09
Summer pub

Tiergartenquelle
6 Bachstraße
3 ☎ 92 76 15
Honest pint,
authentic atmosphere

Café Rix, Neukölln

Vapiano
5 Potsdamer Platz
☎ 23 00 50 05
Help yourself,
fresh Italian food

■ Neukölln

Alte Ratsklause
27–28 Donaustraße
☎ 53 06 55 13
Local Berlin atmosphere

Café Hofperle
131–133 Karl-Marx-Straße
☎ 56 82 94 29
Perfect for brunch

Café Rix
141 Karl-Marx-Straße
☎ 686 90 20

Der kleine Buddha
14 Mareschstraße
☎ 26 32 36 69
Organic café

Der Silberlöffel
21 Maybachufer
☎ 62 90 00 43
Café-bar by canal

Jimmy Woo
24 Friedelstraße
☎ 0176 25 35 62 05

Louis
5 Richardplatz
☎ 681 02 10
Austrian local

Mariamulata
88 Wildenbruchstraße
☎ 0163-918 95 97
Spanish brunch buffet

Nansen
39 Maybachufer
☎ 66 30 14 38
Laid-back,
great cocktails

Rudimarie
34 Weichselstraße
☎ 46 64 46 64

s…Kultur
1 Erkstraße
☎ 61 39 63 61

■ The Outer Edges

Alte Fischerhütte
136 Fischerhüttenstraße
Zehlendorf
☎ 80 49 83 10
Lakeside idyll,
20 minutes from
Krumme Lanke

Alter Dorfkrug Lübars
8 Alt-Lübars
Reinickendorf
☎ 92 21 02 30
Village pub

Alter Krug
52 Königin-Luise-Straße
Dahlem
☎ 832 70 00
Historic inn, Biergarten

Blockhaus Nikolskoe
15 Nikolskoer Weg
Wannsee
☎ 805 29 14
Beautiful lake views,
perfect in summer

Bolles Bootshaus
58b Am großen Wannsee
Wannsee
☎ 80 58 76 42
With lakeside decking area

Bürgershof
4–5 Waldmüllerstraße
Potsdam Klein-Glienicke
☎ 0331 237 88 89

Café Lenné
15a Altensteinstraße
Dahlem
☎ 832 29 273

Café Paulines
1 Theatergasse
Karlshorst
☎ 77 90 85 30
Good cakes,
historic setting

Die Weisse Villa
10 Josef-Nawrocki-Straße
Friedrichshagen
☎ 64 09 56 46
Mansion by Müggelsee

Forsthaus Paulsborn
90 Hüttenweg
Grunewald
☎ 818 19 10
Traditional restaurant,
edge of forest

Gasthaus Majakowski
63 Majakowskiring
Pankow
☎ 49 91 82 50
Dream garden, pretty villa,
GDR history

Goldener Greif
36 Königstraße
Wannsee
☎ 805 40 00

Luise Restaurant-Biergarten
40 Königin-Luise-Straße
Dahlem
☎ 841 88 80
Popular pub,
tables under trees

Mutter Fourage
15a Chausseestraße
Wannsee
☎ 80 58 32 83
Courtyard café,
Mediterranean feel,
good organic food

Ratskeller
21 Alt-Köpenick
Köpenick
☎ 655 51 78
Historic cellar in town hall

Reinhard's Landhaus
56 Königsallee
Grunewald
☎ 895 38 00
In upmarket suburb 30

Restaurant Fährhaus
15 Im Saatwinkel
Tegelort
☎ 35 13 27 97
Waterside setting

Restaurant Waldhütte
Schwarzer Weg
Tegel
☎ 433 48 88

Spandauer Zollhaus
1 Möllentordamm
Spandau
☎ 333 48 41
Historic customs house,
traditional German

Strandlust
3a Seddinpromenade
Müggelsee
☎ 675 86 26
Good for fish.
Converted barge

Waschhaus
19 Katzengraben
Köpenick
☎ 65 49 83 19
Bavarian food,
waterside terrace

Billy Wilder's, Tiergarten

Wirtshaus zur Pfaueninsel
100 Pfaueninselchaussee
Wannsee
☎ 805 22 25

Wirtshaus Moorlake
6 Moorlakeweg
Wannsee
☎ 805 58 09
Lakeside setting,
Old Berlin

■ Bars

al2 cocktail bar
83 Pfalzburgerstraße
Charlottenburg
☎ 88 91 79 60
Smooth lounging

Amano Bar
43 Auguststraße
Mitte
☎ 8094150
Trendy hotel,
great cocktails,
roof terrace

Bar Tausend
11 Schiffbauerdamm
Mitte
☎ 41 71 53 96
Hyped, hedonistic

Becketts Kopf
64 Pappelallee
Prenzlauer Berg
☎ 0162-237 94 18
Cool ambience,
dream cocktails

Billy Wilders
2 Potsdamer Straße
Potsdamer Platz
☎ 26 55 48 60
Cocktails and light meals

CSA Bar
96 Karl-Marx-Allee
Friedrichshain
☎ 29 04 47 41
Former Czech airline
offices

Club der Visionäre
2 Am Flutgraben
Kreuzberg
☎ 69 51 89 42
Cool waterside café/club,
opens midday

Die Tagung
29 Wühlischstraße
Friedrichshain
☎ 29 77 37 88
Local dive bar with
GDR theme

40 Seconds Club
56 Potsdamerstraße
Tiergarten
☎ 890 64 20
Penthouse bar,
360° views, R'nB
and house music

Gainsbourg
5 Savignyplatz
Charlottenburg
☎ 313 74 64
American style, French
soul, old Berlin square

Green Door
50 Winterfeldtstraße
Schöneberg
☎ 215 25 15
Berlin retro-chic,
happy hour 6–8pm

Harry's New York Bar
15 Lützowufer
Tiergarten
☎ 254 78 86 33
Piano bar, great cocktails

Hefners Lounge
146 Kantstraße
Charlottenburg
☎ 31 01 75 20
Pre or après dinner lounge bar

Jansen Bar
71 Gotenstraße
Schöneberg
☎ 0175-712 31 73
Local haunt

Kirk
75 Skalitzer Straße
Kreuzberg
☎ 69 53 52 99
Vibrant and inclusive

Kosmos
131 a Karl-Marx-Allee
☎ 40 04 81 30

Hotel de Rome
37 Behrenstraße
Mitte
☎ 460 60 90
Roof terrace (until sunset)
has great views

Kaffee Burger
58/60 Torstraße
Mitte
☎ 28 04 64 95
Famed for Russian Disco,
ex-GDR hang-out

Nachbar
12 Maaßenstraße
Schöneberg
☎ 23 63 90 59
Friendly, reasonable prices

Newton Bar
57 Charlottenstraße
Mitte
☎ 202 95 40
Newton nudes on wall,
pavement heaters

Roberta Bar
7 Zionskirchstraße
Mitte
☎ 44 05 55 80
DJs play mellow music

Rum Trader
40 Fasanenstraße
Wilmersdorf
☎ 881 14 28
Unique, small 70s bar,
Weimar panache

Sanatorium 23
23 Franfurter Allee
Friedrichshain
☎ 42 02 11 93
Hip lounge,
historic Stalinist
palazzo

Saphire Bar
31 Bötzowstraße
Prenzlauer Berg
☎ 25 56 21 58
Elegant leather sofas,
good cocktails

Slumberland
24 Goltzstraße
Schöneberg
☎ 216 53 49

Times Bar
9 Fasanenstraße
Charlottenburg
☎ 31 10 30
Classic cocktails,
Cuban cigars,
Savoy Hotel

Berlin boasts many legendary bars

Trompete
9 Lützowplatz
Tiergarten
☎ 23 00 47 94
Stylish bar co-owned by German actor

Universum Lounge
153 Kurfürstendamm
Charlottenburg
☎ 89 06 49 95
Slick bar in 1920s Bauhaus gem

Weinerei
57 Fehrbelliner Straße
Mitte
☎ 440 69 83
Pay what you want, wine bar

Würgeengel
122 Dresdner Straße
Kreuzberg
☎ 615 55 60
Faded elegance in the 'Avenging Angel'.

Victoria Bar
102 Potsdamer Straße
Schöneberg/Tiergarten
☎ 25 75 99 77
Great cocktails, tasty light food

Vox Bar
Grand Hyatt Hotel
2 Marlene-Dietrich-Platz
Tiergarten
☎ 25 53 17 72
Live soul, jazz and blues

Zeitlos
64 Kurfürstendamm
Charlottenburg
☎ 88 92 20 35
Great for post-shopping cocktails or after-show drinks

Buy, Buy Berlin

The Berlin shopping scene is full of surprises and offers a real mix of something for everyone. Shopping is not a religion – malls are not the size of cathedrals and very little is open on Sundays. The exclusive brand names are mostly on Friedrichstraße or the Ku'damm but Mitte and Prenzlauer Berg have the coolest local designer shops. Charlottenburg is known for its antiques and art, Kreuzberg for vintage clothes and Schöneberg for home accessories. But wherever you go you have to remember that many shops still don't take credit cards.

Most places open between 9am and 10am. Supermarkets open earlier and smaller fashion boutiques and specialist shops might not open until midday. About four times a year, shops are allowed to trade on Sunday afternoons, and Advent Sundays are also legal shopping days. Closing time is generally 6pm although some shops don't shut until 8pm or later on Friday and Saturday. Supermarkets close generally by 10pm. Outside these hours there are small grocery stores called 'Spätkauf' ('late buy') dotted around the city, as well as the local Turkish or Asian shops. The pharmacy in the Hauptbahnhof (main station) is open 24/7.

Berliners love to buy fresh bread every day and fruit and vegetables from markets. Bakeries are open as early as 6am and usually on Sunday mornings too or all day if there's a café attached. Each Berlin neighbourhood enjoys a once- or twice-weekly visit from stallholders selling fruit and vegetables, meats and cheeses and all sorts of organic produce. Some food markets are much bigger affairs and include arts and crafts stalls as well. At weekends there are wonderful antique and flea markets all over the city.

Main shopping areas

Friedrichstraße Mitte

Glitzy, gritty Friedrichstraße was the epitome of 1920s Berlin. It was decimated in the war and only partly rebuilt afterwards. When the Wall went up, the southern end was severed by Checkpoint Charlie and the East Berlin side remained derelict for years. After reunification, money was poured

Potsdamer Platz Arkaden, Tiergarten

into restoring economic vitality to this lifeless and gloomy section of the street and now the buzz of pre-war days has returned. The Friedrichstadt-Passagen is an exclusive development with three 'quartiers', underlining the French connection with this part of Berlin. Quartier 207 is a spectacular branch of Galeries Lafayette, the Parisian department store, and features a central glass cone. Quartier 206 is an exclusive mall in an art deco setting and leads into Quartier 205 with a large international food hall. Behind the Quartiers, the streets around the Gendarmenmarkt have some interesting independent shops. There are car showrooms on Friedrichstraße and Unter den Linden with vintage models, art exhibits and restaurants and two excellent bookshops nearby, The Berlin Story and Dussmann das KulturKaufhaus.

Kurfürstendamm and Tauentzienstraße Charlottenburg

Berlin's most famous shopping mile has the most diversity in terms of style as well as price. The fabulous KaDeWe department store on Wittenbergplatz is a must for its food hall and entrance hall displays and Tauentzienstraße is crammed with popular fashion stores. The best part of the Ku'Damm is the stretch between Meinekestraße and Adenauerplatz where there is a branch of every international label under the sun and some great individual and specialist shops in the side streets too.

Tauentzienstraße with sculpture 'Berlin', Charlottenburg

Hackescher Markt/Scheunenviertel Mitte
This is the most central area for individual and designer shops. The streets north of Hackescher Markt have become a magnet for indie designer labels, outrageous shoes and edgy accessories, especially the shops on and around Alte Schönhauser Straße between Weinmeisterstraße and Rosa-Luxemburg-Platz stations.

Alexanderplatz Mitte
Although the original Alexanderplatz has been razed to the ground, the post-war Stalinist version has regained much of its character as a down-to-earth, bustling commercial centre. Berliners on a budget come here to shop, especially at Kaufhof, C&A and the Alexa Shopping Mall. The trams are still clanging up and down the streets alongside the square and there are often markets or exhibitions on the open space.

Potsdamer Platz Arkaden Tiergarten
This medium-sized shopping mall has an entrance at lower ground level directly from the Potsdamer Platz S-Bahn station. There is a good mix of over 130 shops arranged over three floors and the building has a light and airy feel to it.

Buy, Buy Berlin

Shopping for Art Schöneberg

Berlin's latest gallery ghetto, the 'Potsdamer Kunstkiez', has developed on and around Potsdamer Straße, in an area known as Tiergarten Süd. The Tagesspiegel complex at 81 Potsdamer Straße, once home to Berlin's great daily newspaper, has been transformed into vast halls housing large galleries and quirky little alleys lead to smaller ateliers. The galleries in the unrenovated building of the Freies Museum Berlin at 91 Potsdamer Straße showcase political and experimental art and there are more treasures tucked away in rooms above cheap clothing shops and Turkish vegetable markets. Pohlstraße is worth exploring too and on the last Saturday of the month dedicated art fans can join the Schöneberger Art Walk.

Individual shops

M=Mitte, C=Charlottenburg, S=Schöneberg, P=Prenzlauer Berg, K=Kreuzberg, F=Friedrichshain, N=Neukölln, W=Wilmersdorf

Antiques

Antiquitäten und Mehr
62 Suarezstraße/
5 Mommsenstr., C

Art Deco
51 Grolmannstraße, C

Auktionshaus Kaiserhöfe
51–54 Mittelstraße, M

Bleibtreu Antik
54 Schlüterstraße, C

Deco Arts
6 Motzstraße, S

Kollwitzkabinett
31 Wörther Straße, P

Kunst-a-bunt
39 Wörther Straße, P

Silber und Antik
2 Walter-Benjamin-Platz, C

Books/Magazines

Another Country
7 Riemannstraße, K
Used and new English books to buy and borrow

Bücherbogen
593 Stadtbahnbogen, C
Art and architecture

Do you read me?
28 Augustraße, M
Coffee table books, magazines

Dussmann Kulturkaufhaus
90 Friedrichstraße, M
Open till midnight, large English section

East of Eden
10 Schreinerstraße, F
Rare and second-hand editions

Hugendubel
13 Tauentzienstraße, C
Biggest branch of German chain

Marga Schoeller Bücherstube
33 Knesebeckstraße, C
Founded 1929, great English selection

Pro QM
48–50 Almstadtstraße, M
Art, design, journals, magazines

Saint Georges Bookshop
27 Wörther Straße, P
New and used English books

Friedrichshain bookshop

Schröersche Buchhandlung
7 Langenscheidtstraße, S
Eclectic mix

Walther König
27 Burgstraße, M
Beautiful books

Fashion and Beauty

Altes Textilkaufhaus
93 Boxhagener Straße, F
Young designers

AM 1–3
21–23 Münzstraße, M
Men's fashion in back courtyard

Awear
75 Kastanienallee, P
Streetwear

Belladonna
101 Bergmannstraße, K
Natural beauty products

Berlinerklamotten
www.berlinerklamotten.de
Berlin arbiter of fashion

Blush, Balls
22 Rosa-Luxemburg-Straße, M
Luxury underwear, both sexes

Budapester Schuhe
199 Kurfürstendamm, C
Shoes for the well-heeled

Chelsea Farmer's Club
50 Schlüterstraße, C
English-style fashion

Cherry Bomb
32 Oranienstraße, K
Young designer labels

Civilist
13 Brunnenstraße, M
Hip men's clothing

Claudia Skoda
35 Alte Schönhauser Straße, M
Handmade knitwear

Crines Design
38 Kurfürstendamm, C
Classic and elegant Berlin style

Buy, Buy Berlin

Eisdieler
12 Kastanienallee, P
Multi-label urban fashion

Extrafein
116 Torstraße, M
Jeans and music

Frau Tonis Parfum
13 Zimmerstraße, M
Personalised scent

Greta & Luis
15 Rosenthaler Straße, M
22 Akazienstraße, S
Multi-label, men and women

Harry Lehmann
106 Kantstraße, C
Nostalgic, fragrances since 1926

Heimzucht
10 Danziger Straße, P
Cleverly chosen fashion

IC! Berlin
17 Max-Beer-Straße, M
Great name, fashionable specs

Jil Sander
185 Kurfürstendamm, C
German designer label

Jünemanns Pantoffeleck
39 Torstraße, M
Felt slippers since 1908

Lunettes
11 Marienburger Straße, P
Stylish sunglasses

Milk
5 Almstadtstraße, M
Trendy, handmade bags

Ono Koon
51 Winterfeldtstraße, S
Inspirational women's fashion

Prachtmädchen
28 Wühlischstraße, F
Lively, local fashion

Schwarzhogerzeil
28 Mulackstraße, M
Parisian panache

Solebox
16 Nürnberger Straße, W
Best for trainers

Sterling Gold
32 Oranienburger Straße, M
Glamorous dresses

Tausendschön
12 Raumerstraße, P
Popular fashion boutique

The Corner
40 Französische Straße, M
High end fashion, celebrities' favourite

Ute Köhnen
141 Linienstraße, M
Handmade jewellery

Yi-Spa
3a Monbijouplatz, M
Relaxing massages

Food and Drink

Absinthdepot
4 Weinmeisterstraße, M
The world of the Green Fairy

Bonbonmacherei
32 Oranienburger Straße, M
Traditional sweet factory

Confiserie Melanie
4 Goethestraße, C
Handmade truffles and chocolates

Confiserie Orientale
113 Linienstraße, M
Turkish sweets

Dong Xuan Center
128 Herzbergstraße, Lichtenberg
Take the M8 tram east to Little Vietnam

Erich Hamann KG
17 Brandenburgische Straße, W
Fine chocolate since 1928

Fassbender & Rausch
60 Charlottenstraße, M
Fine chocolate and café

Goldhahn & Sampson
9 Dunckerstraße, P
Posh deli

Kadó Lakritzfachgeschäft
20 Graefestraße, K
Liquorice, all sorts

Kochhaus
1 Akazienstraße, S
Deli and recipes

Mitte Meer
42 Kantstr., C/
50 Invalidenstraße, M
Mediterranean

Paasburg's Wein
3 Fidicinistraße, K
Wines, spirits,
English spoken

Rogacki
145 Wilmersdorfer
Straße, C
Huge deli started in 1928

Schokogalerie
35 Große Hamburger
Straße, M
For chocoholics

Wald-Königsberger-Marzipan
54a Pestalozzistraße, C

Whisky & Cigars
8–9 Sophienstraße, M

Galleries

Berlin Art Projects
33 Mehringdamm, K
www.berlinartprojects.de

Camera Work
149 Kantstraße, C
www.camerawork.de

Galerie Albrecht
78 Charlottenstraße, M
www.galeriesusannealbrecht.de

Galerie Arndt
96 Potsdamer Straße, M
www.arndtberlin.com

Galerie Eigen+Art
26 Auguststraße, M
www.eigen-art.com

Galerie Ingeborg Vagt
60 Fasanenstraße, C
www.galerie-ingeborg-vagt.de

Galerie Listros
33 Kurfürstenstraße, M
www.galerie.listros.de

galerie OPEN
18–20 Legiendamm, K
www.galerie-open.net

Galerie Sandmann
139–140 Linienstraße, M
www.artsandmann.de

janinebeangallery
154 Torstraße, M
www.janinebeangallery.com

Kunstsaele
90 Bülowstraße, S
www.kunstsaele.de

Klosterfelde
93 Potsdamer Straße, M
www.klosterfelde.de

LEE galerie BERLIN
172 Brunnenstraße, M
www.leegalerieberlin.com

Michael Schultz
Contemporary Art
34 Mommsenstraße, C
www.galerie-schultz.de

MORGEN CONTEMPORARY
27 Oranienburger Straße, M
www.morgen-contemporary.com

Gifts and souvenirs

Ach Berlin
39 Markgrafenstraße, M
Tasteful Berlin gifts

Ampelmann Shops
37 Markgrafenstraße, M
Fun goods designed around the iconic dumpy East German traffic light men (also in Hackesche Höfe, DomAquarrée, Potsdamer Platz Arkaden)

Aus Berlin
17 Karl-Liebknecht-Straße, M
Berlin souvenirs

Herrlich
2 Bergmannstraße, K
Gifts for men

Vorwende-Laden
16 Thaerstraße, F
GDR mementoes

O.K. Versand
36/37 Alte Schönhauser Straße, M
From every continent

Buy, Buy Berlin

Lifestyle

Coledampf's Culturzentrum
39 Wörther Straße, P
Kitchenware

Galerie Filmposter.net
21 Pücklerstraße, K
Movie posters

Glasklar
13 Knesebeckstraße, C
Drinking glasses

Green Living
36 Schönhauser Allee, P
Ecological furnishings

Grüne Erde
1–3 Oranienburger Straße, M
Natural products

Kaufbar
4 Gärtnerstraße, F
Everything is on sale in this café-bar

Kwikshop
44 Kastanienallee, P
Petrol station-style hatch

KPM Königliche Porzellanmanufaktur
1 Wegelystraße, M
White porcelain in historic factory site

RSVP
14 Mulackstraße, M
Exquisite stationery

Stilwerk
17 Kantstraße, C
Emporium of design shops

Villa Harteneck
9 Douglasstraße, Grunewald
Interior design in mansion setting

Zwischenzeit
35 Raumerstraße, P

Music/Records

DNS Recordstore
30 Eberswalder Straße, P
Club music

Dussmann das KulturKaufhaus
90 Friedrichstraße, M
Best for classical and jazz

Gelbe Musik
11 Schaperstraße, C
Avant-garde outlet

Hard Wax
44a Paul-Linke-Ufer, K
Knowledgeable, friendly

Melting Point
55 Kastanienallee, M
House, disco

Musikalienhandlung Hans Riedel
42 Uhland Straße, C
Classical scores

Mr Dead and Mrs Free
5 Bülowstraße, S
Indie

Sameheads
10 Richardstraße, N
Run by three English brothers

Traditional Toys and Games

Heidi's Spielzeugladen
61 Kantstraße, C

Kinderkaufhaus
140 Torstraße, M

Onkel Albert
63 Zionskirchestraße, M

Onkel Philipps Spielzeugwerkstatt
35 Chorinerstraße, P

Ratzekatz
7 Raumerstraße, P

Viel Spiel
28 Große Hamburger Straße, M

Vintage wear

Colours
102 Bergmannstraße, K

Garage
2 Ahornstraße, S

Made in Berlin
19 Neue Schönhauserstraße, M

Trash-Schick
31 Wühlischstraße, F

Saturday market entertainment on Kollwitzplatz, Prenzlauer Berg

Markets

The market scene is full of colour and life unique to Berlin and the atmosphere is witty and warm-hearted. The Berlin Senate has over 170 markets on its lists, clear proof of the Berliners' love of this form of shopping.

Food markets

Kollwitzplatz Prenzlauer Berg
Neuer Markt (New Market) Saturdays 09:00–16:00
Öko-Markt (Organic Market) Thursdays 12:00–19:00
There is plenty of purchasing power here and organic products sit side-by-side with more exotic fare. On Saturdays there are stalls selling arts and crafts and plenty of stops for wine-tasting and gourmet snacks as well as beer and currywurst. In summer live music adds to the weekend feeling and it's easy to fall in love with pretty 'Prenzlberg'.

Hackescher Markt Mitte
Thursdays 09:00–18:00 and Saturdays 10:00–18:00
The market outside Hackescher Markt station has more stalls on Saturdays, but it's always fun browsing for food specialities and hand-made accessories and gifts.

Karl-August-Platz, Trinitatiskirche Charlottenburg
Wednesdays 08:00–13:00, Saturdays 08:00–14:00
At this market the age profile is older. The Charlottenburg bourgeoisie are looking to spoil themselves with flowers and plants, home-made jams, perfumed soaps and exotic cooking oils. You may even spot Sir Simon Rattle queuing for tomatoes. At midday there is a 20 minute church service in the Trinitatiskirche, an old market tradition.

Winterfeldtplatz Schöneberg
Wednesdays 08:00–14:00, Saturdays 08:00–16:00
The clientele is more mixed here. The Schöneberger middle classes rub shoulders with a younger crowd among a wider choice of arts and crafts stalls selling exotic fabrics and hand-made jewellery. The food stalls are similar to elsewhere, with plenty of organic products. In May the scent of lilac fills the air.

Hohenzollernplatz Wilmersdorf
Wednesdays and Saturdays 08:00–13:00
This is a small market for lovers of tradition. The flowers, fruits and vegetables and household wares are set out by the church steps. At midday you can enjoy the sacred music of 'Noonsong' at the Church Hollenzollernplatz.

BiOriental Türkenmarkt am Maybachufer Neukölln
Tuesdays and Fridays 11:00–18:00
At this huge authentic Turkish Market on the banks of the Landwehrkanal the fresh produce is at bargain prices and there are spices that can't be found anywhere else west of Istanbul. More exotic still are the Red Sea sponges, silk fabrics, burkas and Arabian cosmetics and perfume. Turkish housewives are out in force, buying their supplies for the week ahead, jostling with the local in-crowd and tourists.

Markthalle Neun Kreuzberg
Fridays 12:00–19:00, Saturdays 09:00–16:00
This is a new initiative in one of Berlin's historic market halls. It is billed as 'seasonal, regional and international'.

Market on Winterfeldtplatz, Schöneberg

These four markets are also worth browsing if you are in the area. They are all in pretty locations and popular with locals for fresh produce:
Farmers' Market, Zionskirchplatz Mitte Thursdays 11:00–18:00
Weekly Market, Arkonaplatz Mitte Fridays 12:00–19:00
Organic Market, Chamissoplatz Kreuzberg Saturdays 09:00–15:00
Weekly Market, Schlachtensee Zehlendorf Tuesdays 08:00–14:00
and Wednesdays 08:00–14:00

Arts, Crafts, Antiques and Flea Markets
Trödelmarkt an der Straße des 17. Juni Tiergarten
Saturdays and Sundays 10:00–17:00
This is Berlin's biggest 'antique' market. The German word 'Trödel' means 'junk' in English, but many of the goods here are genuine antiques and fans of old silver, porcelain, glass and linen will have a field day. Some of the stallholders are authentic Berlin 'characters' who have been trading here for decades and others are just selling off jumble. Bargaining is the order of the day and you can pick up pretty vintage jewellery and interesting bric-a-brac for a couple of euros.

Flohmarkt am Mauerpark Prenzlauer Berg
Sundays 08:00–18:00 (or till sunset in winter)
This massive flea market has the largest selection of trendy clothes and accessories, but you may have to rummage through a lot of jumble to find the perfect vintage buy. Bargaining is expected and can be spirited. Don't miss the afternoon entertainment in the small Mauerpark amphitheatre. In February 2009, an Irish ex-pat bicycle courier plugged in a portable karaoke set here and created a stage for anyone with the guts to sing and dance in public. Now 'Bearpit Karaoke' attracts huge crowds on fair weather Sunday afternoons.

Trödelmarkt am Arkonaplatz Mitte
Sundays 10:00–16:00
Just across the road from Mauerpark is Arkonaplatz where the stalls are laid out under the shade of the lime trees. This square is the place for that special vintage Berlin buy – an art deco lamp, a china doll or a fine wine glass. The market scene here was captured by Heinrich Zille in 1912 and the cobbled streets with their old lamps and street signs have a nostalgic feel.

Trödelmarkt am Boxhagener Platz Friedrichshain
Sundays 10:00–18:00
Lots of private sellers make this a good market for bargains. It is round the corner from the centre of Friedrichshain's pub scene and is frequented by a younger crowd. The stalls reflect their tastes with a good choice of vinyls, CDs and trendy fashion gear as well as the usual East Berlin 'junk'. Live music completes the scene.

Großer Antikmarkt am Ostbahnhof Friedrichshain
Sundays 09:00–17:00
This 'antique' market deserves its name, although there are fewer on offer than at the 'junk' market on Straße des 17. Juni. The stalls are set out on the north side of the Ostbahnhof and the goods for sale here have a solid, pre-war Berlin feel to them; bread tins, embroidered tea towels and china ornaments. The stallholders are friendly and happy to haggle.

Kunstmarkt am Zeughaus Mitte
Saturdays, Sundays and Public Holidays 11:00–17:00
There are thirty or so stalls in this weekend arts and crafts market on Kupfergraben opposite Museumsinsel. Prices are generally not negotiable.

Arkonaplatz flea market, Mitte

Antik- und Buchmarkt am Bodemuseum Mitte
Saturdays, Sundays and Public Holidays 11:00–17:00
Only a hundred metres further on, past the Pergamonmuseum, is another collection of stalls on the cobbled street opposite the Bode-Museum. Here discerning buyers carefully search among old books, pictures and postcards and antique porcelain, silver and glass. The Currywurst van under the railway bridge or the cafés under the arches in Georgenstraße make a good refreshment stop.

Trödelmarket auf dem John-F-Kennedy-Platz Schöneberg
Saturdays and Sundays 08:00–17:00
Trödelmarkt auf dem Fehrbelliner Platz Wilmersdorf
Saturdays and Sundays 09:00–16:00
Both these markets are in the western part of the city where the neighbourhoods are generally wealthier. If you look carefully, you might find a piece of pretty antique porcelain or something of historic interest. The stallholders here are likely to manage a few words of English and with a bit of flattery, the price can be knocked down even further.

Buy, Buy Berlin

The Berlin Calendar

The Berlin year is crammed full of events. This city thrives on festivals and fairs, parades and carnivals and uses any excuse for a celebration or a demonstration. Seasons are important too; Berliners hit the beaches and the beach bars in summer and know how to turn the big freeze to good use. There are regular annual fixtures and plenty of extras thrown in. To keep ahead of the game it is best to check the Berlin online calendar:
| www.visitberlin.de/en/experience/events/event-calendar

Main Events

New Year's Eve
- **Berlin Open End** – Fireworks at the Brandenburg Gate (and everywhere else)

January
- **Grüne Woche** – International food fair
- **Bread and Butter** Fashion fair, Tempelhof Airport (also in July)
- **Six Day Cycling** Tempodrom

February
- **Transmediale** – Festival of Media Art
- **Lange Nacht der Museen** – Long Night of the Museums, one night at the beginning of February over 90 museums stay open until midnight or later.
- **Berlinale** – International Film Festival

March
- **März Musik** Classical concerts

April
- **Berlin Half** Marathon

May
- **May Day** Street parties and riots in Kreuzberg
- **Myfest** Festival in Kreuzberg
- **Karneval der Kulturen** in Kreuzberg, street fair celebrating diversity

June
- **DMY** – International Design Festival
- **Fête de la Musique** – Concerts all over Berlin
- **Berlin Gay and Lesbian Festival** at Nollendorfplatz
- **Christopher Street Day (CSD)** Gay and Lesbian parade

Christmas Market on Gendarmenmarkt, Mitte

July
- **Classic Open Air** – Gendarmenmarkt
- **Berlin Klassiktage** – Classical music in historic settings

August
- **Beer Festival** – Karl-Marx-Allee
- **Lange Nacht der Museen** – (see February)
- **Tanz im August** – International dance festival
- **KulturBrauerei Summer evening** – Concerts with fireworks
- **Heimatklänge** – World-music festival at Tempodrom
- **Young Euro Classic** – Konzerthaus

September
- **Pyronale** – Spectacular two-night pyrotechnic event
- **Popkomm** – International music fair
- **Musikfest Berlin** – The world's greatest orchestras
- **Berlin Marathon**

October
- **Art Forum Berlin** – 100 international galleries
- **Tag der Deutschen Einheit** – 3rd October German public holiday
- **Festival of Lights** – Illuminations and Laser beams on iconic buildings

November
- **JazzFest**
- **Jewish Cultural Days**

December
- **Christmas Markets** transform the capital into a winter fairyland. Among the best are Domäne Dahlem, Gendarmenmarkt, Opernpalais, Rixdorf, Schloss Charlottenburg and Sophienstraße. Details at www.visitberlin.de/en.

Best Beaches
- **Badeschiff an der Arena**
  4 Eichenstraße
  12435 Berlin-Treptow
  www.arena-berlin.de/badeschiff
  Swimming pool in the Spree. Relax in hammocks or deckchairs

- **Strandbad Wannsee**
  25 Wannseebadweg
  14129 Berlin-Zehlendorf
  www.strandbadwannsee.de
  Most popular beach in Berlin for over 100 years

- **Freibad Müggelsee**
  838 Fürstenwalder Damm
  12589 Berlin-Köpenick
  East Berlin's counterpart to the Wannsee

- **Sommerbad at the Insulaner**
  80 Munsterdamm
  12169 Berlin-Steglitz
  Outdoor pool in beautiful green surroundings

- **Strandbad Tegel**
  21 Schwarzer Weg
  13505 Berlin-Tegel
  www.strandbad-tegel.de
  Second largest lake, great sand

- **Flughafensee**
  Betzdorfer Pfad
  13507 Berlin-Tegel
  Clean quarry pond north of Tegel Airport

- **Schlachtensee** and **Krumme Lanke**
  14129 Berlin-Zehlendorf
  Best lakes in the Grunewald, with ducks and fish

- **Weißensee**
  174 Berliner Allee
  13088 Berlin-Weißensee
  Lake among trees, evening swimming

Best Beach Bars

- **Beach at the Box**
  21–23 Englische Straße
  10587 Berlin-Tiergarten
  www.beachberlin.com

- **Ku'damm Beach**
  5a–b Königsallee
  14193 Berlin-Charlottenburg
  www.kudammbeach-berlin.de

- **Oststrand**
  24 Mühlenstraße
  10243 Berlin-Friedrichshain
  www.strandbar-mitte.de

- **Ressort**
  50–51 Invalidenstraße
  10557 Berlin-Tiergarten
  www.ressort-berlin.de

- **Traumstrand**
  6a Friedrich-List-Ufer
  10557 Berlin-Tiergarten
  www.traumstrand-berlin.de

- **Überseebar**
  155 Berliner Allee
  13086 Berlin-Weißensee
  www.binbaden.de

- **Yaam**
  35 Stralauer Platz
  10243 Berlin-Friedrichshain
  www.yaam.de

Winter

This is the time to hit the ice rinks of Berlin. Indoor rinks (Eislaufbahn) are listed at www.schlittschuhe.net/schlittschuhlaufen-berlin. In the city centre there are temporary outdoor rinks by the Neptunbrunnen under the TV tower or at Potsdamer Platz. Another great skating experience is on the roof terrace of the **nhow Hotel** by the Oberbaumbrücke. You don't need to be a hotel guest to use this rink which has fantastic views across the Spree (www.nhow-hotels.com/berlin).

Jewish Berlin

The story of Jewish Berlin will tragically be forever linked to the horrors of the Holocaust. In central Berlin there are three main Jewish sites of remembrance: the Memorial to the Murdered Jews of Europe, the Neue Synagoge and the Jewish Museum, as well as several smaller museums and memorials. In recent years, the threat of neo-Nazi and Islamic terrorist attacks has led to increased police security, but they are there to protect visitors, not to menace. Germany wants to encourage people to visit these Jewish sites and keep the past as a constant memory. The Villa Wannsee in south-west Berlin, where the conference was held which determined the fate of all Jews in Europe, is also dedicated to commemorating the Holocaust. Three further sites that bear witness to Nazi atrocities committed against the Jews, other minorities and opponents of the Nazi regime, are described in 'Hitler's Berlin'.

The History

Jews first arrived in Berlin in the 13th century. They were continually the target of oppression and following their expulsion in 1571, virtually no Jews lived in Berlin for almost a century. This changed in 1663, when Israel Aaron came to Berlin as a court Jew and soon afterwards 50 prosperous Jewish Viennese families were allowed into the city as 'protected Jews'. Despite restrictions the Jewish community grew and by the beginning of the 18th century the Jewish ghetto numbered over 1,000. Although Jews had to pay more in taxes they were excellent merchants and soon among the richest residents in Berlin. Philosopher and scholar Moses Mendelssohn arrived in Berlin in 1743 and urged Jews to integrate into secular life.

In 1815 the Jews gained Prussian citizenship and by 1850 they had full equality. At the turn of the century, the number of Jews in Berlin had grown to about 110,000. Wealthier Jewish families started to move to the outer districts and Jewish institutions thrived. The Weimar Republic (1919–33) was the golden age of German Jewry and they made a huge contribution to Berlin's cultural life. When Hitler came to power in 1933 there were over

160,000 Jews living in Berlin. The Nazis systematically eliminated their social and economic rights and in June 1938 thousands of Jews were arrested without reason. On the evening of the 9th November, which the Nazis called 'Reichskristallnacht' and is now referred to as 'Pogromnacht', Jewish synagogues and shops were vandalized and burned down throughout Germany. Almost 12,000 Berlin Jews were sent to Dachau concentration camp that night. During the months that followed, more and more Jews were arrested and sent to forced-labour camps. By 1939 many Jews had managed to emigrate and the Jewish population of Berlin stood at just 75,000.

In 1941 much of the city was closed off to Jews, and they had to wear the yellow star. Between 1941 and 1943 all the city's Jews were deported to camps throughout Europe, and on 16th June 1943 Berlin was declared 'judenrein' ('clean of Jews'). By 1945 only 8,000 Jews remained in Berlin – those who had been in hiding or were married to non-Jews. Some of them stayed, mostly in West Berlin, where there was a sizeable community. This was bolstered by an influx of displaced persons at the end of the war, largely from Eastern Europe. When the Berlin Wall fell the Jews of East and West Berlin were united and were joined by thousands of immigrants from the former Soviet Union who strengthened the traditional elements of the community.

Memorial to the Murdered Jews of Europe

This central site of remembrance and commemoration near the Brandenburg Gate has become one of Berlin's most defining symbols. Peter Eisenman's five and a half acre design resembles a sea of 2,711 charcoal-coloured stone slabs or 'stelae', some rising as high as 13 feet. Visitors can enter from all four sides and may lose themselves in the maze as they negotiate the narrow paths between the slightly tilted blocks, treading on the uneven ground beneath their feet. In the south-east corner of the site, there is an underground Information Centre containing a powerful exhibition. Yad Vashem in Jerusalem released the 3.2 million names of Jewish victims of the Holocaust held in their archives and these names and biographies are ceaselessly read out in the 'Room of Names'. Some people find this experience and the personal objects on display more enduring symbols of the atrocities than the abstract art of the memorial itself. Others feel that Eisenman's concept is appropriate precisely because it is an abstraction and does not dictate what the observer should feel. At the very least a walk through this Holocaust memorial is both thought-provoking and unsettling.

| 1 Cora-Berliner-Straße, 10117 Berlin-Mitte, www.stiftung-denkmal.de

Memorial to the Murdered Jews of Europe, Mitte

The Neue Synagoge

The gilded dome and towers of the Neue (New) Synagoge stand out on the skyline making it Berlin's most exotic landmark. When it was consecrated in 1866 it was the largest synagogue in Europe, with 3,200 seats. It was desecrated and set on fire by Nazi Stormtroopers, allied bombing caused further destruction and most of it was demolished in the 1950s. In the mid-1980s the front of the building was restored, but the bulk of the synagogue was never rebuilt. In its place is an empty plot of land with the original layout of the building marked out on it. The Neue Synagoge is run by the Centrum Judaicum and functions mainly as a museum with an exhibition on the history of the building and its congregation which includes original decorative furnishings and a Torah scroll. The only way to access the open space is by joining a guided tour. The Centrum Judaicum also arranges special tours on Jewish life in the area around the synagogue. Sabbath services are held in a modern addition to the Neue Synagoge.

| 29–31 Oranienburger Straße, 10117 Berlin-Mitte, www.or-synagoge.de

The Jewish Museum

This is one of Europe's outstanding museums. But although the persecution of the Jews by the Nazis is so sensitively treated, it should not been seen as a

Holocaust museum. The breadth of the collection leaves the impression there is a much larger story and a rich culture of Jewish life in Germany. This is the history of the Jewish presence in Germany, not German-Jewish history. The exhibitions and collections are in a remarkable building designed by Daniel Libeskind. The opening was planned for the fateful day of 11th September 2001 but was delayed for two days after the terrorist attacks. The zinc-clad structure is shaped like a deconstructed Star of David (the aerial view is stunning) and contains bizarre angles to symbolize the Holocaust. Its purpose is to create a sense of disorientation, interspersed with feelings of claustrophobia and panic, and to convey the horrors of persecution. The baroque building, containing the museum entrance and bookshop, is a former 18th century courthouse, used by West Berlin as the Berlin Museum during the city's division.

The museum's collections are accessible via an underground passage. They chronicle 2,000 years of history of the Jewish community in Germany and on the third floor there is a general overview of Judaism. A second underground tunnel connects the museum to 'The Garden of Exile', with disturbingly tilted foundations. An oleaster grows out of reach, on top of 49 tall pillars. The final underground tunnel leads from the Museum to the Holocaust Tower, a 79 foot tall empty silo, whose only light comes from a small slit in its roof. Complementing Libeskind's striking architecture are some works of contemporary art, notably 'Shalechet' ('Fallen Leaves'). Occupying a corner space called the 'Memory Void', this installation consists of 10,000 iron faces strewn across the floor. The faces are coarsely stamped but full of expression, with mouths open in suffering.

| 9–14 Lindenstraße, 10969 Berlin-Kreuzberg, www.jmberlin.de

Museum Blindenwerkstatt Otto Weidt

During the war Otto Weidt, a partially-sighted broom and brush maker, employed Jewish workers in his workshop in a courtyard behind Haus Schwarzenberg next to the Hackesche Höfe. Weidt tried to protect his mostly blind and deaf employees, bribing the Gestapo, falsifying documents, and eventually hiding a family behind a backless cupboard in one room of his shop. This museum tells Weidt's story, using photos and interviews with some of the people he saved. Tours in English are available free of charge, bookable in advance.

| 39 Rosenthaler Straße, 10178 Berlin-Mitte,
www.museum-blindenwerkstatt.de

Neue Synagoge, Mitte

Stille Helden

In the building next to Otto Weidt's workshop, 'Silent Heroes' pays tribute to the thousands of German gentiles who risked everything to save Jews from persecution and tells the stories of people who spent years in hiding. A total of 5,000 German Jews were saved from the Nazis in this way, 1,700 of them Berliners. The multi-media three-room exhibition in German and English has audio accounts and touch-screen computers describing how they survived. It documents not only the successes in saving Jews, but also the attempts that failed. One of the shadowbox pillars is dedicated to Oskar and Emilie Schindler.

| 39 Rosenthaler Straße, 10178 Berlin-Mitte, www.gedenkstaette-stille-helden.de

Anne Frank Zentrum

Haus Schwarzenberg also contains a museum which recalls the life of Anne Frank. In one room you can read from Anne's diary and look at some of the objects from her daily life. In a second room are colourful wigwams with video installations where young people of today explore their thoughts about their lives and their ambitions, set alongside similar thoughts from Anne Frank. There is a 30 minute film in English about Anne's life.

| 39 Rosenthaler Straße, 10178 Berlin-Mitte, www.annefrank.de

Wir waren Nachbarn
We were neighbours

Rathaus Schöneberg has a permanent exhibition featuring a collection of 136 family albums about former Jewish residents from the borough of Tempelhof-Schöneberg. These moving biographies containing pictures, documents and reports, present an idea of life in Berlin before 1933 and the gradual steps of 'isolation and deprivation of rights, expulsion, deportation and murder of Berlin Jews from 1933 to 1945'. Some of them have an English translation. The exhibition is closed on Fridays.
| John-F.-Kennedy-Platz, 10825 Berlin-Schöneberg

Gedenkstätte Haus der Wannsee-Konferenz
Wannsee Conference Memorial

On 20th January 1942, 15 high-ranking Nazis met at a beautiful lakeside mansion to draw up plans for the 'Final Solution'. Their goal became the extermination of the entire Jewish population of Europe, about eleven million people. Today the Villa Wannsee has been converted into a place of remembrance. The permanent exhibition is a thorough account of the conference itself, including Eichmann's minutes, and the process of deporting Jews to the ghettos and extermination camps. It also addresses the question as to how much the Germans knew about the genocide. The elegant house together with its landscaped gardens was originally built in 1914 by a Berlin industrialist. In 1940 the estate was purchased for the SS Security Service.
| 56–58 Am Großen Wannsee, 14109 Berlin-Wannsee, www.ghwk.de

Jewish memorials

There are many other memorials scattered throughout Berlin. Several are in the area behind Hackescher Markt where Jews originally settled. On Große Hamburger Straße next to the Jewish High School and in front of Berlin's old Jewish cemetery is a stone commemorating the collection point established by the Gestapo in 1942. It was from here, the site of a former Jewish Old People's Home, that 55,000 Berlin Jews started their journey to the death camps. Next to the stone is the 'Memorial for the Jewish victims of fascism', a group of diminished bronze figures who emanate total desolation and seem to be waiting for a train. They are standing in front of the oldest Jewish cemetery in Berlin, destroyed by the Gestapo in 1943. Now a peaceful garden, just one grave has been reconstructed – the tombstone of Moses Mendelssohn

Gedenkstätte Haus der Wannsee-Konferenz, Wannsee

(1729–86), German-Jewish philosopher of the Enlightenment and grandfather of the famous composer. Almost opposite the Jewish High School is a gap between the buildings and on the sides of the walls is the 'Missing House' graphic with the names of the former residents.

At 6 Krausnickstraße is a plaque commemorating the first woman rabbi in the world, murdered in Theresienstadt. Further up Große Hamburger Straße on Koppenplatz is the memorial 'Der verlassene Raum' (The Abandoned Room). A bronze table and two chairs, one of which is thrown upside down, depict a room which the inhabitants were violently forced to leave. Along Auguststraße are several buildings used by the Jewish Community before the war. 17 Auguststraße housed various Jewish welfare institutions between 1895 and 1941. The Jewish Hospital was in a building in the back courtyard of 14–16 Auguststraße from 1861 until 1914. After that it was used for community projects and from 1941–43 it was a Gestapo collection point for old and sick Jewish residents. The red brick building at 11–13 Auguststraße was a Jewish girls' school from 1930 to 1942.

On the other side of Hackescher Markt there are two memorial sites on Rosenstraße, a small street now crammed with ugly post-war buildings. In a small park is the 'Block der Frauen', a sculpture recalling the non-Jewish women who protested for days outside the building at 2–4 Rosenstraße where their Jewish husbands were being held by the Nazis. The men were

Track 17, S-Bahnhof station Grunewald

subsequently released. Most of them survived and their families formed the core of the Jewish community in Berlin after the war. The other memorial marks the site of the Old Synagogue in Heidereutergasse, the very first in Berlin, in use for almost 250 years and also used as a Gestapo collection point before it was destroyed in an air raid.

On Unter den Linden, in the south-east corner of the Lustgarten, is the Herbert Baum Memorial stone. This honours a group of Jewish Communists who attempted to set fire to an anti-Soviet propaganda exhibition on this site in 1942. Baum and his 28 comrades, their families and a further 500 Jews were arrested and murdered. On Bebelplatz is the memorial to mark the Nazi burning of the books, many of them by Jewish writers (page 200). In 2008 a memorial was unveiled outside Friedrichstraße station. A bronze sculpture commemorates the 1.6 million children murdered in the Holocaust and the 10,000 children whose lives were saved by being granted entry into England in 1938. It is one of three 'Kindertransport' sculptures by Frank Meisler, who was saved by one of the trains bound for London from Gdansk. The other two are at Liverpool Street Station, London and the main railway station in Gdansk.

There are several other memorials to the Berlin Jews who left the city by train. At 7 Levetzowstraße in Tiergarten is the site where Jewish citizens were assembled, then marched to Putlitz station. The monument is a wagon

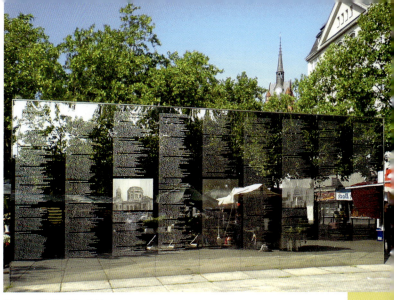

Mirror Wall, Steglitz

loaded with human stone figures, a memorial wall with the details of all transports and memorial plaques to the synagogues set on fire on 'Reichskristallnacht'. A further memorial has been placed in the middle of Putlitz Bridge overlooking the freight yard where thousands of Berlin Jews were herded onto cattle trucks. These deportations are most graphically commemorated at Grunewald S-Bahn Station. A large concrete wall featuring hollow figures stands by the steps leading up to Gleis 17 (track 17). Along the edge of the platform on either side of the track are steel grates listing every transport between 1941 and 1945, the number of people, and their destination. A total of 35,000 Berlin Jews were loaded onto trains here and transported to the death camps in the East.

Other memorials in West Berlin include large plaques inscribed with the names of 12 Nazi concentration camps, for example outside Wittenbergplatz station. The borough of Steglitz has created the Spiegelwand (mirror wall) to commemorate 1,723 Jewish residents who were deported to concentration camps. Their names, addresses and dates of birth are written on a mirror, which reflects the comings and goings on the street outside. Life goes on, but there should be no forgetting. The 'Ort der Erinnerungen' (Place of Memories) in the Bayerisches Viertel in Schöneberg also makes a powerful statement. This neighbourhood had a high proportion of Jewish residents before the war, including Albert Einstein, and 60% of the infrastructure was

Stolpersteine commemorating Hugo and Hertha Klein

destroyed in the bombing. The memorial is a network of eighty signs (in German and English) hanging from street lamps. These are the laws introduced by the Nazis to discriminate against the Jewish population. Some are strategically located to link them to present-day reality. A sign in front of a playground states, 'Aryan and non-Aryan children are forbidden to play together'. The eighty scattered signs are gathered together on three large billboards at Rathaus Schöneberg, Bayerischer Platz and in front of Münchener Straße Gymnasium. Each billboard shows pre- and post-war maps of the area, one from 1933 and the other from 1993. (www.stih-schnock.de)

A very special way of commemorating individual victims of Nazi terror are the 'Stolpersteine' (stumbling stones), single brass cobblestones embedded in the pavement outside the former home of the murdered person. Engraved on the stone are the words 'Hier wohnte …' ('Here lived …') followed by the name of the former resident, their year of birth, the year they were killed and the place of execution. There are well over a thousand in Berlin, all sponsored by local citizens.

Jewish Berlin today

Today, there are over 30,000 Jews living in Berlin. The Jewish Community of Berlin has three centres. The main one is at 79–80 Fasanenstraße, Char-

The Klein's son left Berlin on the 'Kindertransport' and survived

lottenburg (www.jg-berlin.org). The Adass Jisroel Community, in the old Jewish quarter of Berlin, was re-established in 1994 as an independent Jewish Orthodox Community. Its centre is at 40 Tucholskystraße (www.adass-jisroel.de). There are seven synagogues, but it is only possible to visit one if you attend a service or during the 'Days of Jewish Culture' in September. Germany's largest synagogue is in Prenzlauer Berg at 53 Rykestraße. It was the only synagogue for the Jewish Community of East Berlin and the red brick building has been beautifully restored. Also in Prenzlauer Berg, on Schönhauser Allee, is the second oldest Jewish Cemetery in Berlin, opened in 1827 when the Große Hamburger Straße site became too small. There are 22,000 graves here, including those of Max Liebermann and composer Giacomo Meyerbeer. In 1880 when space had run out here too, a new one was inaugurated at Weißensee. This vast and beautiful burial ground is still in use today and contains the imposing tombs and graves of many renowned Berlin Jews. It is open Sundays to Thursdays from 10am until 5pm and on Fridays from 10am until 3pm.

Hitler's Berlin

The German capital is where Hitler consolidated his power, wiped out his rivals, led Germany into war and defeat, then committed suicide. But you have to know where to look to find the legacy of the Third Reich. There are guided tours of Nazi Berlin but they involve a lot of standing around listening to history you may already know, looking at buildings you have already seen or being shown old photographs which are difficult to examine properly in a group. There is also the problem that Nazi Berlin becomes a ghoulish tourist trail. If you strike out on your own you have more thinking time, can select what interests you most and restore morale when necessary by stopping for a break. The places which link the Nazi terror regime exclusively with the fate of the Jews are included in 'Jewish Berlin'.

Nazi Buildings

Wilhelmstraße runs from Pariser Platz in front of the Brandenburg Gate into Kreuzberg, a distance of about two kilometres. Originally a wealthy residential street with a number of palaces belonging to members of the Prussian royal family, it developed into the main government district from the mid-19th century. From 1875 the Reich Chancellery building stood at 77 Wilhelmstraße. During the years of the Weimar Republic (1919–33), the Reich President's official residence was at 73 Wilhelmstraße. It was from the balcony of this building that Reich President Paul von Hindenburg watched the torchlight parade on the night the Nazis came to power.

In 1938–39 a new Reich Chancellery was built for Adolf Hitler by Albert Speer. Completed in 1938 after only 11 months, it had vast proportions, long corridors and used quarry loads of red marble. This building stood immediately south of the old Chancellery and its official address was 4 Voßstraße, although the balcony from which Hitler addressed crowds faced Wilhelmstraße. Hitler's new Chancellery was badly damaged in the bombing and the remains were demolished in the early 1950s. Much of the marble and stone was used to make the Soviet war memorials and for the reconstruction of Mohrenstraße station nearby. The square opposite the building, known as

Information board at Gertrud-Kolmar-Straße, Mitte

Wilhelmplatz, no longer exists. Also vanished is the Kaiserhof Hotel which was Hitler's favourite residence in Berlin before he came to power.

Although the ruins of both the old and the new Chancellery were levelled by the Soviets, Hitler's bunker largely survived. Since 1945 government authorities have been anxious to avoid it becoming a Neo-Nazi shrine and have kept the surroundings anonymous. Attempts to destroy it proved difficult because of its thick concrete roof and as it was located within the border installations, the site remained neglected for many years. When it was developed, the immediate area was surrounded by a parade of shops and a car park was built over the emergency exit point for the bunker. In June 2006, when the World Cup was held in Germany, an information board was erected with a plan of the bunker to mark its location at the corner of In den Ministergärten and Gertrud-Kolmar-Straße.

During the Nazi era, the German Foreign Office was situated at 73 Wilhelmstraße, in the former Reich President's Palace. The Finance Ministry stood at 61 Wilhelmstraße and Goebbels' Propaganda Ministry stood further south at 8–9 Wilhelmstraße. The Agriculture Ministry occupied the site at 72 Wilhelmstraße as it still does today, the only German government ministry located on its pre-war site, although in a reconstructed building. The British Embassy was at 70 Wilhelmstraße and its ultra-modern successor was built on this site after reunification. The Berliners have given it the nick-

Reich Air Ministry building at Wilhelmstraße in 1938

name 'Das bunte Haus' (the colourful building). The only major surviving public building from the Nazi era is Goering's Reich Air Ministry building at 81–85 Wilhelmstraße. Formidable, stark and massive, it is a perfect example of how Nazi architecture was designed to make the individual feel small in comparison to the power of the state. During the GDR era it became the 'Haus der Ministerien' and was the focal point for demonstrators during the workers' uprising on 17th June 1953. There is a GDR mural and a memorial at the Leipziger Straße end of the building. After reunification it was taken over by the German Finance Ministry and was used by Treuhand, the agency which sold off East German property and companies. Apart from the former Air Ministry, all the major public buildings in the government district were severely damaged by Allied bombing. The GDR regime had the ruins demolished in the early 1950s. It was not until the 1980s that apartment blocks were built along this section of the street. There are several useful information panels along Wilhelmstraße, showing where the well-known buildings of the pre-war era once stood and giving their history.

Third Reich architecture

Hitler wanted buildings which expressed the might of Germany and its national cultural traditions. A monumental style for public buildings became the order of the day and the ideal models were the Greek temple, the Renaissance palace, the Baroque castle and the Classicist building of the Imperial era. For domestic housing a 'folksy' style was favoured, a perfect example is the 'Waldsiedlung Krumme Lanke' a settlement in Zehlendorf built in the 1920s and later occupied by SS officers and their families.

Nazi architecture in Berlin consisted of two phases. The first included the party edifices and a number of other giant structures still in use today, for example Zoologischer Garten station and the Olympia Stadion. But it is Tempelhof Airport that best conveys the grandiose proportions of monumental Nazi architecture, described by British architect Sir Norman Foster as 'the mother of all airports'. The terminal building, built between 1936 and 1941, forms a massive 1.2-kilometre long quadrant. Passengers walked through customs into a dazzlingly huge, simple and light-filled reception hall. Tempelhof finally ceased to operate as an airport in 2008, but the buildings are under a preservation order and currently host fairs and festivals. Once the focus of the famous Berlin airlift, this 950 acre site has now been transformed into a public park and in 2013 it is to undergo a four-year, 60-million-euro facelift.

The second phase of Nazi architecture was the future plan for Berlin, Nuremberg and Munich, the key cities of the Third Reich. Albert Speer was entrusted with the project for Berlin, 'World Capital Germania', the ultimate architectural realisation of National Socialist ideology. In 1938, Speer finished the design for the first part of the north-south axis, an avenue 4 miles long, flanked by 400 streetlights. In 1925, Hitler had sketched a triumphal arch to dwarf the Eiffel Tower and a gigantic assembly hall. These plans were never realised, although buildings were demolished and streets widened in preparation. However, part of the east-west axis which already existed in Prussian times gives a hint of its promised grandeur and many of Speer's street lamps flank its sides. The Siegessäule which dominates this stretch of road originally stood in front of the Reichstag, but was moved in 1939 as part of the Germania plan.

Air-raid shelters

In the end the buildings erected by the Nazis had to include defences and protection against allied bombing. After the RAF's minor raid on Berlin in 1940, Hitler ordered the construction of three massive flak (anti-aircraft gun) towers which were also used as above-ground bunkers and as civilian shelters. Berliner Unterwelten (www.berliner-unterwelten.de) runs guided

Air-raid shelter, Gesundbrunnen station, Mitte

tours through the remaining flak tower in the Humboldthain park and through the air-raid shelters under Gesundbrunnen station. The air-raid shelter under the Gruselkabinett near Anhalter Bahnhof (www.gruselkabinett-berlin.de) shows original film footage of the bombing. In 1941 the Nazis decided to build bunkers above ground because it was cheaper. Over 1,000 were built and the remains of around 350 can still be seen dotted around the city.

Resistance

There are two main memorial sites in Berlin which honour the citizens who resisted the Nazi regime, most of whom had to pay for their courage with their lives.

The Gedenkstätte Deutscher Widerstand (German Resistance Memorial Centre) is in the 'Bendlerblock' on Stauffenbergstraße near Potsdamer Platz. During the Third Reich this building housed the Wehrmacht High Command and it was here that Colonel Claus Schenk Graf von Stauffenberg and his associates plotted to kill Hitler and then stage a coup d'état. On 20th July 1944, von Stauffenberg attended a military briefing at Hitler's headquarters in East Prussia and left an explosive device in a briefcase. But the assassination attempt failed and that same evening the conspirators were executed by firing squad in the courtyard of the Bendlerblock. In 1953 this courtyard was dedicated as a memorial to German resistance and in 1955 Bendlerstraße was renamed Stauffenbergstraße. A permanent exhibition on resistance against the Nazi regime is on display on the second floor of the Bendler Block. English speakers should book a guided tour as most of the documentation is in German.

| www.gdw-berlin.de

The Gedenkstätte Plötzensee (Plötzensee Memorial Centre) was set up to honour the memory of all the victims of the Third Reich and in particular the 3,000 who were executed at Plötzensee Prison in Wedding between 1933 and 1945. The execution chamber was a small brick outhouse and visitors can see inside the room where in a single night in September 1943 186 people were hanged from butchers' wire in groups of eight at a time. Between 180 and 200 conspirators in the July Plot were put to death, 89 of them at Plötzensee. A small exhibition documents the cruelty of the Nazi judicial and penal system and tells the story of several brave resistance groups. A visit to Plötzensee is a harrowing experience but it is also a pilgrimage. Most German schools organise visits to memorials and former concentration camps for their older pupils to ensure that they are aware of the nature and extent of the crimes committed during the Third Reich. Outside the execution chamber is a large stone wall with an inscription commemorating the victims of the 'Hitler Dictatorship' and nearby stands a large urn containing earth from concentration camps.

| www.gedenkstaette-ploetzensee.de

Topographie des Terrors

This outstanding new exhibition tells the story of the Nazi terror machine operated from the Gestapo and SS Headquarters, right next to the hub of political power in Wilhelmstraße. The buildings were destroyed in the war and then demolished, but they once housed the offices of Heinrich Himmler, Leader of the SS, Reinhard Heydrich, Director of the Reich Security Office and Adolf Eichmann who organised the mass deportation of Jews. It was from here that the concentration camps were administered, plans for the Holocaust were finalised, the military taskforces were managed and detailed records of the Nazi regime's opponents were kept. In the prison cells thousands of people were held and often tortured before being sent to concentration camps.

After the war West Berlin did not develope the site because it was so close to the Berlin Wall. It was left as wasteland until 1987 when a citizens'

Topographie des Terrors, Tiergarten

initiative started work on preserving it. Now a new two-storey steel and glass rectangle houses the grim story of this corner of Berlin. There are scores of photographic displays documenting the history of Nazi atrocities and one wall is full of file cards with the identities of some of the operators of the Nazi killing machine. Typically they were ambitious academics in their 30s who were keen to climb the career ladder and few of them were ever prosecuted. The site tour integrates remains of the Berlin Wall and follows the exposed building remnants. There are 15 stations with information displays about the site's history and its use during the Nazi period and the post-war era. Alongside the excavated segments of the cellar wall is a permanent exhibition about Berlin during the Third Reich. Entrance to both the exhibition and grounds is free.

| www.topographie.de

Sachsenhausen Memorial and Museum

This former concentration camp is on the outskirts of Oranienburg, just to the north of Berlin, but easily accessible by S-Bahn (tariff C) followed by a twenty minute walk from Oranienburg station – the same route that many of the prisoners were forced to take. The camp was built during the Olympic Games in 1936 and of the 200,000 people held here during the Third Reich, tens of thousands never survived. During the Olympics the Nazi propaganda machine managed to cover up the fact that all opponents and 'enemies' of the regime were being systematically interned all over Germany in camps like Sachsenhausen.

The camp is on a triangular plot designed by SS architects for about 6,000 inmates. The entrance building is the cold stone reality of the image most people have engraved in their mind, complete with a harmless-looking clock tower and a wrought-iron gate containing the cruelly untrue words 'Arbeit macht frei' ('work will free you'). Surrounded by a 2.6-metre-high wall with watchtowers and an electrified barbed-wire fence, the prisoners' barracks were spread out like a fan in four rows. There were many other buildings and facilities outside the camp, including a brick-works where camp inmates had to make bricks for the monumental buildings of Speer's future 'world capital Germania' and the headquarters for the central administration of the entire concentration camp system.

Sachsenhausen served as 'a preventive detention camp' where the Gestapo sent political opponents of the Nazi regime as well as those persecuted for racial, religious or social reasons. When the war started the Nazis brought prisoners from other countries to Sachsenshausen and in 1941 the SS murdered over 10,000 Soviet prisoners of war here. Sachsenhausen was not originally intended as an extermination camp and in 1942 large numbers of Jews were relocated to Auschwitz, but the construction of a gas chamber and ovens in 1943 facilitated the means to kill larger numbers of prisoners. 30,000 inmates died in Sachsenhausen from exhaustion, disease, malnutrition or pneumonia. Many others were executed or died as the result of brutal medical experimentation. When the war was over the Soviets interned captured Nazis in the barracks and the suffering and death continued for a further five years.

The GDR government started work on the Sachsenhausen National Memorial in 1957 and in 1993 the Sachsenhausen Memorial and Museum was created. The visitors' centre at the entrance has a model of the camp and the surrounding buildings. It is still possible to visit the original prisoners' laundry room, the kitchen, the infirmary and a pathology building. Visitors can walk through part of the former cell block, where the Gestapo tortured and murdered the inmates, as well as barracks 38 and 39, referred to as the 'Jewish Barracks'. Just outside the camp there are detached houses where more prominent prisoners were kept and a new pavilion housing the Soviet Special Camp Museum. The former Station Z which contained an execution site and a small gas chamber and crematorium is also outside the main

Sachsenhausen Memorial, Oranienburg

camp. In total there are 13 permanent exhibitions at Sachsenhausen with details of specific features of the camp, including prisoners' documents and personal items. You can either walk round the site on your own or join a guided tour. Mosaic Tours is a non-profit making organisation that conducts regular tours of Sachsenhausen. In their brochure they quote the words of Elie Wiesel, survivor of Auschwitz:

"Remembering is a noble and necessary act. If anything can, it is memory that will save humanity."

| www.stiftung-bg.de

Memorial for Homosexuals

In May 2008, on the edge of the Tiergarten opposite the Holocaust Memorial, a memorial was unveiled to commemorate all the homosexuals who died at the hands of the Nazis. The four-metre-tall concrete block has a small window revealing a black and white film of two men kissing. An inscription reads, "A simple kiss could get you in trouble." Hitler's regime was profoundly homophobic. Over 100,000 gay men were registered on police lists, called 'pink lists', and it is estimated that over 10,000 of them perished in concentration camps.

The burning of the books

In the middle of Bebelplatz on Unter den Linden is a window on the surface of the cobbled square. Beneath it is the memorial to mark the site where on 10th May 1933 the Nazis staged a symbolic burning of books. Over 2,000 books blacklisted by the Nazis were burned on the square. These included books written by 'non-Aryans', such as Jews, Poles or Africans as well as books that had an anti-Nazi message. The 'Bibliothek' memorial was created by Israeli artist Micha Ullman and consists of empty bookshelves with the exact dimensions to hold all the burned books. It can only be viewed through glass from above and is especially effective at night. Two bronze plaques either side of it contain lines written by Heinrich Heine in 1820 which originally referred to the Spanish Inquisition: 'Das war ein Vorspiel nur. Dort wo man Bücher verbrennt, verbrennt man auch am Ende Menschen' (That was only a prelude. Where they burn books, they ultimately burn people).

Berlin-Schöneweide
Documentation Centre on Nazi Forced Labour

The Nazis abducted approximately 12 million people from almost twenty European countries and housed them in labour camps near large armament factories. Many workers died as a result of their living conditions, mistreatment, malnutrition, or became civilian casualties of war. The last well-preserved former Nazi forced labour camp in Berlin is in Schöneweide, South Berlin. Eleven of the original thirteen housing barracks at Schöneweide are still standing and two of them have been turned into exhibition and seminar spaces.

| www.topographie.de

Russia remembers

The Soviet victory in the Battle for Berlin saw the end of Hitler's Third Reich and the occupation of the city by the Red Army before the other wartime Allies arrived. But victory came at a huge cost to the Soviets and 20,000 of them fell in the attack on Berlin. Just a few months after the end of the war a Soviet War Memorial was erected on the edge of the Tiergarten near the Reichstag, in an area which was the scene of particularly heavy fighting (page 48). But Berlin's most spectacular war memorial is the 'Sowjetisches Ehrenmal' built from 1946 to 1949 in the gardens of Treptower Park using stone and marble taken from Hitler's new Chancellery building. Visitors

Soviet War Memorial, Tiergarten

walk up towards the memorial area between two fifteen-metre high triangular forms in red granite and look across a central area lined on both sides by 16 stone sarcophagi, one for each of the 16 Soviet Republics with relief carvings of military scenes and quotations from Joseph Stalin. This area is the final resting place for some 5,000 soldiers of the Red Army. The focal point of the memorial is the towering statue of a Soviet soldier. He is standing on a mausoleum on the top of a grassy hill, symbolically slicing a smashed swastika. He is holding a child he has saved and is staring out across the graves. At the other end of the Memorial is a moving sculpture of 'Mother Russia' mourning her lost sons.

Divided Berlin

In 1945 the victorious powers couldn't agree on the future of the German capital and among the bombed-out ruins there was a growing clash between political systems. The end result was the setting up of two new German states and between 1949 and 1961 millions of East Germans used the 'loophole' of West Berlin as a means of emigrating to the West. Then the Berlin Wall went up overnight and the Cold War started in earnest. Daily life continued, but it took different forms on either side of the Wall. The one similarity was that each half of the city was in the international spotlight and was used as a showcase by its political masters. East Berlin was the pride of the Eastern Bloc and West Berlin received huge subsidies from West Germany to attract residents, business and tourists. Now that Berlin has been reunited for over 20 years it is difficult to see that it once contained two worlds, even if the Soviet-style architecture in East Berlin tells its own story. In recent years there has been an upsurge in 'Ostalgie', a nostalgia for the dubious trappings of the GDR years, which has led to a rash of shops and restaurants selling the designs and food of this era. There are also several museums specifically devoted to life in the divided city.

DDR Museum

This museum advertises itself as 'a hands-on experience of everyday life in the GDR'. It is crammed with exhibits and there are drawers and cabinets full of objects and scenes unique to the socialist state. The displays about aspects of daily life such as the workplace, schools, young communist groups and holidays all have a distinctly nostalgic feel. There is a mock-up of the inside of a typical GDR flat, visitors can sit at the wheel of a Trabant and take a simulated ride through communist East Berlin, complete with all the authentic exhaust smells, or sit in GDR cinema seats and watch propaganda films of smiling East Berliners. There is also a second, newer part of the exhibition which is not such a cosy affair. Visitors pass through a smoke-screen with pictures projected onto it and move from everyday life into the state machine of the GDR. This was a grimmer world where one political

A nostalgic 'Trabi' ride through Berlin

party (SED) controlled all the instruments of power and its Ministry of State Security (Stasi) had a whole nation under surveillance. In the Domklause next door you can sample dishes from the GDR regions surrounded by GDR style décor and the ubiquitous communist slogans of that time.

| 1 Karl-Liebknecht-Straße, 10178 Berlin-Mitte, www.ddr-museum.de

Stasi Museum

This is the real McCoy, a museum in the former headquarters of the GDR's State Security Service. In 1989 there were 8,000 employees working in this huge complex of buildings. Haus 1 contained the offices of Erich Mielke, infamous Head of the Stasi from 1957 to 1989. His study, conference room, secretaries' offices and cafeteria were all left unchanged after reunification. Among the most fascinating exhibits are the examples of the weird and wonderful ways that the Stasi found to spy on their fellow citizens; camouflaged briefcases, a watering can, a dustbin, a pen, a tree trunk, a mini-camera designed to look like a coat button and even a fake rock. If you have seen the film 'The Lives of Others' you will recognise the jars containing fabric used for collecting and preserving people's scents. A guided tour in English is recommended and some of the guides have their own personal stories to tell about the Stasi.

| 103 Ruschestraße, Haus 22, 10365 Berlin-Lichtenberg, www.stasimuseum.de

GDR-style architecture on Alexanderplatz, Mitte

Gedenkstätte Berlin-Hohenschönhausen

A visit to the former Stasi prison in Hohenschönhausen is not for the fainthearted. In the early 1990s, former inmates took up the cause of turning the prison compound into a memorial. The vast majority of the buildings, equipment, furniture and fittings have survived intact and a visit to Hohenschönhausen gives an authentic picture of prison conditions in the GDR. It is only possible to look round the prison itself by joining a group tour which includes the underground cells. Tours are often led by former inmates, who provide chilling first-hand details of prison conditions. There are daily tours in English.

The memorial also features one or two interesting exhibitions. During the Soviet occupation at the end of the war, German prisoners were sent to the Gulags from Hohenschönhausen and many more died of starvation and exhaustion. The Stasi inherited the site from the Soviet administration in 1951 and soon afterwards used it to incarcerate members of the democratic workers' uprising on 17th July 1953. The Stasi ran other operations from here on the site, including a workshop for forgeries and the Espionage Data Processing Centre (HVA). Much of the area around the prison was a forbidden zone for East Berliners and until 1974 Labour Camp X next to the prison was for inmates sentenced to forced labour.

| 66 Genslerstraße, 13055 Berlin-Hohenschönhausen, www.stiftung-hsh.de

Checkpoint Charlie today

Stasi – Die Ausstellung

A new exhibition of the records kept by the Stasi opened on 15th January 2011 on Zimmerstraße near Checkpoint Charlie. 21 years earlier on 15th January 1990, East German activists stormed the redundant Stasi headquarters and managed to salvage a significant proportion of the vast numbers of files, recordings and photos in the Stasi archives. Former Stasi officers had been in the process of destroying the material and some 16,000 bags with already shredded documents were also retrieved. Since the archives were opened up 20 years ago, there have been almost three million requests from people wanting to read what Stasi spies wrote about them. Alongside the personal case histories, the exhibition examines the structure and history of the Stasi and the methods they used. The organisation was obsessed with recording the mundane details of everyday lives and gathered much of its information with the help of a network of 100,000 unofficial collaborators, in a country of 16 million people.

| 90 Zimmerstraße, 10117 Berlin-Mitte

Tränenpalast Palace of Tears

In September 2011 Angela Merkel, the German Chancellor, opened a new permanent exhibition in the odd-shaped pavilion building just outside Fried-

Tränenpalast, Friedrichstraße, Mitte

richstraße Station which served as the border crossing for visitors travelling to and from East Berlin by train or U-Bahn. The exhibition is called 'Border Experiences. Everyday life in East Germany' and among the items on display are the original customs booths, telephones and surveillance TVs as well as Stasi training films, letters exchanged between divided lovers, countless photos and suitcases full of East German memories. There are LCD and audio stations with English language options but it's best to get to this exhibition early to avoid the queues later in the day. Admission is free and it is proving a very popular attraction with Berliners from both sides of the city. Frau Merkel grew up in the GDR and after walking round the exhibition she recalled her own sad farewells to her grandmother from the West when she always wondered if she would see her again. The authenticity of the Tränenpalast exhibition conveys the harsh reality of life in East Berlin and the obsessive bureaucracy of the GDR regime.
| 17 Reichstagufer, 10117 Berlin

Alliiertenmuseum Allied Museum

This is the only museum in Berlin specifically devoted the western half of the city and tells the story of the Western Allied powers and Berlin during the period from 1945 to 1994. The museum is in the former American Sector on

Alliiertenmuseum, Zehlendorf

Clayallee, Dahlem and named after Lucius D. Clay, US Military Governor in Germany from 1947 to 1949. Clay was seen as the 'father' of the Berlin Airlift by the West Berliners. On the opposite side of the road are the former headquarters of the Supreme Command of the Berlin Brigade and nearby on Hüttenweg was 'Truman Plaza', the huge American forces shopping centre.

The museum is in two buildings – the Outpost Theater, built by the US Army in 1952/53, and the Nicholson Memorial Library, built in 1979. On the tarmac between them stands a Dakota DC8, one of the aircraft used in the Airlift, known as 'Rosinenbomber' (Sultana Bombers) among the West Berliners. Behind the Dakota is a carriage from the American military train which ran to Frankfurt every day during the Cold War in order to keep that rail corridor open. The main exhibition is organised chronologically starting with the moment the three Western Powers marched into their Berlin sectors after the German defeat and ending with the common euphoria at the fall of the Berlin Wall and German reunification. The Outpost Theater contains the first part of the collection and centre stage is a mammoth exhibition on the Berlin Airlift (1948/49). The diaries and letters written by the Americans and British stationed in Berlin after the war make fascinating reading.

The Nicholson Memorial Library tells the second half of the story; the events leading up to the building of the Wall and the role of the Allies as

Sculpture 'The day the Wall came down', Zehlendorf

'Protecting Powers'. There are plenty of larger exhibits on display here including the original Checkpoint Charlie hut and a section of the 'Spy Tunnel'. The Allied Museum has to keep a third of its exhibits in storage, including a number of larger objects. These include a historic British Hastings reconnaissance plane which is in a hangar at Tempelhof, together with a second French plane.
| 135 Clayallee, 14195 Berlin-Zehlendorf, www.alliiertenmuseum.de

Erinnerungsstätte Notaufnahmelager Marienfelde
Marienfelde Refugee Center Museum

Between 1949 and 1990, four million people left East Germany (GDR) for West Germany (FRG) and several refugee centres were set up in West Berlin. 1,350,000 of them passed through Marienfelde, opened in 1953 in southwest Berlin. The refugees were housed and cared for here and went through the process required to obtain a residence permit for West Germany and West Berlin. The Center has been turned into a museum and the fascinating exhibition documents individual stories.
| 66/80 Marienfelder Allee, 12277 Berlin-Marienfelde,
www.notaufnahmelager-berlin.de

The Berlin Wall

For 28 years the East German government insisted that the Berlin Wall was an 'Anti-Fascist Protection Wall' and it was being constantly strengthened and extended. Behind the frontline concrete barrier was the death strip (Todesstreifen) – a 100-metre-wide zone of fences, guard dog tracks, anti-vehicle trenches, alarms, observation towers and often a further rear wall. The middle section was manned by border guards who had orders to shoot and kill if anyone attempted to cross the city's divide. As late as 1989, Erich Honecker proclaimed that the Wall would remain for 100 years. Then, quite suddenly, in the wake of mass demonstrations in East Germany, the Wall was breached as quickly and decisively as it had been erected.

Today it seems incredible that such a bizarre construction was able to survive so long. Very few sections of the Wall remain standing and most traces of it have been entirely obliterated. The Geschichtsmeile Berliner Mauer (Berlin Wall History Mile) is a permanent public exhibition consisting of thirty information panels positioned along the route of the Wall in the city centre. A double row of cobblestones interrupted by copper plates with the inscription 'Berliner Mauer 1961–1989' have been set into the street surface where the Wall once stood, and by the Reichstag building concrete plates as wide as the base of the Wall mark its route. There is also a wall path along the entire former border strip for walkers and cyclists. It runs along the former guard road and sometimes follows the customs border path that was used by the western security forces. Maps and information panels have been erected along the route marked officially as the 'Berliner Mauerweg'.

There are still some places in Berlin where you can get an idea of what the 'border installations' actually looked like. The most authentic and historically significant piece of the Wall has been preserved at Bernauer Straße which is now the site of the official Wall Memorial. This whole area is of immense historic importance. The longest section of remaining Wall has been turned into the 'East Side Gallery' which runs along the Spree between Ostbahnhof and Oberbaumbrücke and it is also well worth walking along the route of the Wall through the city centre .

Bernauer Straße, Mitte

Bernauer Straße

As the barbed wire and bricks went up in August 1961, one side of this historic street was in the borough of Wedding in West Berlin and the other was in Pankow in East Berlin. Many of the residents risked their life attempting to jump into the West from the top windows of the houses while the lower ones were being sealed up. Film evidence of these scenes was shown all over the world. Now Bernauer Straße has become the central point of remembrance and has an increasing number of interesting sites and exhibitions. The best place to arrive is Nordbahnhof S-Bahn station. During Berlin's division this was one of the 'Geisterbahnhöfe' (ghost stations) and there is an interesting exhibition in the entrance area. West Berlin underground maps labelled these stations "Bahnhöfe, auf denen die Züge nicht halten" (stations at which the trains do not stop) and East Berlin maps excluded them altogether. The area opposite the S-Bahn station has been developed into an urban park. It was once a section of the border strip built on the former grounds of the main Nordbahnhof station demolished in the mid-1950s.

At 119 Bernauer Straße a Visitors' Centre supplies helpful information and has a good bookshop. As you walk up Bernauer Straße, you soon come to the first part of the Berlin Wall Memorial (Gedenkstätte Berliner Mauer). A short stretch of the border has been reconstructed here, incorporating the front wall, the rear wall and the death strip in between, complete with an

East Side Gallery, Friedrichshain

original watch tower. A little further along is the modern Chapel of Reconciliation (Kapelle der Versöhnung), also an important part of the Memorial, consecrated on 9th November 2000 and built on the site of the former Church of Reconciliation which was stranded in the middle of 'no man's land' and demolished by the GDR authorities in 1985. Regular services are held in the Chapel to recall the individual stories of people who died at the Berlin Wall. The surrounding area has been developed into parkland dotted with information boards and memorials.

The Documentation Centre on the opposite side of the road at 111 Bernauer Straße is the third part of the Berlin Wall Memorial. The tower has a viewing platform recalling the more simple edifices of Cold War days when people climbed wooden steps to stare incredulously over the border strip into East Berlin. The exhibition inside the Centre is even more gripping. It is entirely possible to spend several hours here studying the displays and historic film footage. Admission is free but the centre is closed on Mondays.

| www.berliner-mauer-gedenkstaette.de/en

East Side Gallery

It is only thanks to an artistic accident of history that the East Side Gallery is one of the few sections of the Wall still standing. It snakes along the River

Spree for about 1.3 kilometres and was created a few months after the fall of the Wall in November 1989 by an international group of artists who wanted to express their reactions visually. Some of the murals have become iconic images, like the Trabant car that appears to burst through the Wall and the 'brotherly kiss' between Leonid Brezhnev and Erich Honecker. Many of the murals bear slogans of peace and they all warrant a closer look.

The East Side Gallery is across the road from the Ostbahnhof. This was the station where during the war hundreds of thousands of German soldiers boarded trains bound for the Eastern front. The Ostbahnhof was featured in the 2004 film, The Bourne Supremacy. Jason Bourne is seen parking his car here, entering the station and leaving a bag in a locker. On the left of the Ostbahnhof is the Postbahnhof, a partially bombed-out complex of railway buildings and warehouses originally built to handle incoming and outgoing mail for the whole of the German Reich. In the GDR years it was used by the Stasi who opened all letters and packages sent from abroad. Now some of the buildings have been turned into exhibition spaces or club venues with bare red-brick vaulted roofs and rusting iron girders.

Cross over the main road (Mühlenstraße) and the East Side Gallery is in front of you. Technically the Gallery covers a section of the 'Hinterlandmauer' (rear wall) not an actual 'Grenzmauer' (border wall), which in this case was the River Spree itself. This section of the rear wall runs along the former GDR protocol route and was built to look like the front wall so that foreign diplomats were spared a view of the death strip. In GDR days Mühlenstraße carried very little traffic and the pavement by the wall was deserted. Now the East Side Gallery is one of Berlin's most popular tourist attractions. Over the years the murals suffered considerable damage from weather erosion, graffiti and tourists who chipped off pieces to take home as souvenirs, but in 2009 they were fully restored for the 20th anniversary of the fall of the Wall. The river bank behind the Gallery has also been transformed from a derelict strip of wasteland into an attractive area, complete with beach bar.

The amazing wall paintings stretch eastwards almost as far as the Oberbaumbrücke, the iconic bridge which links Friedrichshain and Kreuzberg, two Berlin boroughs once divided by the Wall. It was built in 1732 as a wooden drawbridge as part of the excise wall on the city boundary and served as a gate to the city. Its name means 'upper tree bridge' and originated from the heavy tree trunk covered in metal spikes used as a boom to block the river at night to prevent smuggling. A new bridge was opened in 1896 at the time of Berlin's great industrial expansion complete with the two towers as a reminder that the site was once Berlin's river gateway. In April 1945 the

Oberbaumbrücke, Kreuzberg/Friedrichshain

Wehrmacht blew up the middle section of the bridge in an attempt to stop the Red Army from crossing it. It was temporarily rebuilt in 1950 and in August 1961 it became part of East Berlin's border with West Berlin. From December 1963 onwards, the Oberbaumbrücke was used as a pedestrian border crossing for West Berlin residents and for old-age pensioners from East Berlin who were allowed free access to the West, and became known as 'Pensioners' Bridge'. The bridge has been restored to its former glory, given a new steel mid-section and was opened to pedestrians and traffic on the fifth anniversary of the fall of the Wall. Since 1997 it has featured a permanent neon installation called 'Stein-Papier-Schere' (scissors-paper-stone). According to the artist the elements of the two randomly-generated neon signs are symbolically engaged in a constant game that has neither winners nor losers.

As you walk along the East Side Gallery towards the bridge there is a landing stage by the Spree for sightseeing boat trips. During the Cold War this stretch of river was heavily patrolled by border guards and underwater grating prevented any attempts to swim across to West Berlin. On 11th May 1975, five-year-old Çetin Mert drowned on the West Berlin bank of the Spree south-west of the Oberbaumbrücke; he had fallen into the river and GDR border guards refused to let West Berliners rescue him. The East Side Gallery ends by some souvenir stands and there are riverside cafés and a floating hotel, the Eastern Comfort Ship. On the other side of the main road is the new O_2 World, a temple of entertainment on the wasteland of Cold War Berlin. At Warschauer Straße station you can pick up the U1, but it is worth walking across the Oberbaumbrücke to enjoy the views of the old Berlin docks and warehouses, especially towards sunset.

| www.eastsidegallery.com

Tracing the Wall in the city centre

Checkpoint Charlie was the military border post used by all foreigners and diplomats entering East Berlin. This was where Soviet and US tanks confronted each other in October 1961 while politicians wrangled over Allied military access to East Berlin. The original hut is now on display at the Alliiertenmuseum but has been replaced by a copy. The area around it has an excellent permanent open-air exhibition as well as the inevitable souvenir shops and street vendors. On the corner of Kochstraße is the Mauermuseum (opened in 1962) which is crammed with exhibits and tells the story of the Wall and the many daring escape attempts. Many of them failed. If you turn right into Zimmerstraße and cross over Charlottenstraße, a memorial stele marks the place where 18-year-old Peter Fechter bled to death while trying to escape over the Wall in 1962. A Berlin Wall History Mile board gives all the tragic details.

To start your 'Wall Tour', return to Checkpoint Charlie and continue along Zimmerstraße towards Niederkirchnerstraße. Here there is a 160-metre-long stretch of Wall on the border between the Berlin boroughs of Kreuzberg and Mitte. This part of Berlin was the heart of the Nazi government apparatus and behind the preserved Wall is the Topographie des Terrors, described in 'Hitler's Berlin'. Bear right into Stresemannstraße and on the corner with Köthener Straße you will pick up the line of cobblestones marking the Wall. They lead across Leipziger Platz where there are two more sections of rear wall and behind the office blocks on the left is one of the five remaining watch towers out of 300 once interspersed along the Berlin Wall.

The huge complex of modern buildings now dominating the skyline is the new Potsdamer Platz. When the Wall was erected in 1961, the eerie wasteland around Potsdamer Platz was suspended in time and was a favourite stopping point for coach-loads of tourists eager to see over the Wall into 'no man's land'. On the corner of Ebertstraße, in front of Potsdamer Platz station, are individual sections of the Wall and usually two men wearing the uniform of the former Volkspolizei (People's Police), offering tourists 'original East German visa stamps'. The cobblestones in the ground now extend

Marked path of the Wall at Brandenburg Gate

along Ebertstraße to the Brandenburg Gate, clearly marking the Wall's path. Today the whole area around the Brandenburg Gate is teeming with tourists but during Berlin's division the Wall ran right in front of its columns and neither East nor West Berliners had direct access to it. On 9th November 1989, when reports came in that the border restrictions had been lifted, this was where the crowds headed to celebrate and an extra border crossing had to be opened.

The Wall continued along the eastern side of the Reichstag building. The southern bank of the River Spree belonged to West Berlin, while the water itself was on East Berlin territory. In 1971, on the tenth anniversary of the construction of the Wall, a group of West Berlin citizens established the 'Weiße Kreuze' (White Crosses) memorial site at the point where the outer wall met the riverbank. The crosses were inscribed with the names of the fugitives who had died or been killed in their attempt to escape and their dates of death. The original crosses are now on the edge of the Tiergarten on the corner of Scheidemannstraße and there is a new installation of seven crosses by the Spree. A Berlin Wall History Mile board on Reichstagufer tells the story of the "Weiße Kreuze" memorial. On Scheidemannstraße another board describes how the Reichstag building was affected by the Wall.

There are several more interesting sites on the 'East Berlin' bank of the Spree. The first is the 'Parlament der Bäume' (Parliament of Trees) a memo-

White crosses by the Spree

rial for the people who died at the Berlin Wall, set up by the artist Ben Wargin in 1990. To reach it you have to cross the Spree over the Marschallbrücke to Schiffbauerdamm. The installation of trees, memorial stones, original parts of the border fortifications, pictures and texts is in the grounds of the Marie-Elisabeth-Lüders-Haus, the Bundestag library building. It is open on Fridays, Saturdays and Sundays. Further along the Spree at Invalidenstraße was a border crossing point for residents of West Berlin. Günter Litfin was shot and killed near here on 24th August 1961 as he attempted to swim across the Spree, making him the first victim of the Wall. Barriers were subsequently lowered into the water to deter others, while patrol boats monitored the entire network of waterways. At Sandkrugbrücke Bridge a sign recalls the abortive escape attempt made by 12 young men and women in 1963.

On the eastern side of the Spandau navigation canal there is a new walkway leading to Invalidenfriedhof. This cemetery was once the final resting place of prominent Prussians, but only a few of the older grave sites remain – many of them were levelled to make room for the 'death strip', rather a macabre stroke of fate. The rear wall and parts of the asphalted truck strip that runs through the cemetery have been preserved and are now listed as historical monuments. There is an information panel in the cemetery grounds, documenting two deaths: those of Günter Litfin and Peter Göring,

... and back to the Hauptbahnhof

a border soldier, accidentally shot in May 1962 when West Berlin police tried to offer 14 year old Wilfried Tews covering fire during his escape to the West. A little further on, to the north of the cemetery on Kieler Straße, is an old watch tower standing forlorn in front of a new residential complex. Bus 120 on Scharnhorststraße will take you back to the Hauptbahnhof, one of the defining symbols of a reunited Berlin.

Berlin Timeline

c. 700 A.D. Slav tribes settle on the land which later becomes Berlin.
1237 Berlin's sister town, Cölln, is first mentioned in a document.
1244 Berlin is first mentioned in a document.
1443 The first Stadtschloss (City Palace) is built on the banks of the Spree.
1618–48 Berlin loses a third of its population in the Thirty Years War.
1685 The Edict of Potsdam grants the immigration of Huguenots, Protestant refugees from France, who settle mainly in Berlin.
1740–86 Friedrich II (Frederick the Great) is King of Prussia and has many famous buildings constructed in Berlin.
1791 The Brandenburg Gate is opened to the public.
1806 French occupation troops under Napoleon march into Berlin.
1871 The German Empire is proclaimed, with Berlin as its capital.
1902 Berlin is the fifth large European city to have an underground railway.
1919 The Spartacus uprising and murder of Karl Liebknecht and Rosa Luxemburg.
1920 Greater Berlin is founded, consisting of seven urban and 59 rural communities.
1933 Adolf Hitler celebrates his election as Reichskanzler (Imperial Chancellor) with a torchlight procession through the Brandenburg Gate.
1936 The Berlin Olympic Games are used by the Nazis for propaganda purposes.
1938 Anti-Jewish Pogrom during the night of 9th/10th November, 'Reichskristallnacht'.
1944 Resistance fighters are arrested and executed following the failed 20th July assassination attempt on Hitler.
1945 Hitler commits suicide in his Berlin bunker on 20th April. Berlin capitulates to the Soviets on 2nd May. Berlin is divided into four Allied Sectors.
1948 The Soviet blockade of the Western Sectors and the start of the Berlin Airlift.

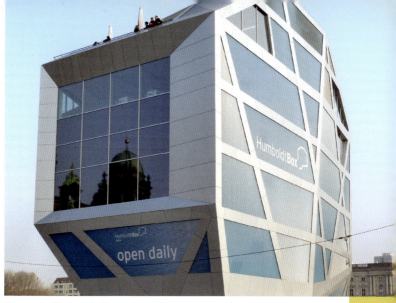

Visit the Humboldt-Box and see into Berlin's future

1949	Two separate German States are founded. The Federal Republic has Bonn as its capital and East Berlin is the capital of the German Democratic Republic.
1953	Soviet troops are used to quell the workers' uprising on 17th June in East Berlin.
1961	The Berlin Wall is erected on 13th August.
1989	Erich Honecker resigns as leader of the SED and the GDR. On 9th November the checkpoints are opened and the Wall falls.
1991	The Bundestag in Bonn decides to move the German capital to Berlin.
1999	The first sitting of the Bundestag in the restored Reichstag building.
2001	The 23 Berlin boroughs are amalgamated into 12 boroughs.
2001	The Jewish Museum opens its doors to the public.
2006–08	The Palast der Republik (GDR parliament building) is demolished.
2008	US President Obama visits Berlin on 24th July.
2009	The 'Neues Museum' is reopened on 16th October and all five museums on Museumsinsel (Island of Museums) are once again open to the public.
2011	Berlin commemorates the 50th Anniversary of the building of the Wall.

Berlin Timeline

Acknowledgements

I would like to thank everyone who has accompanied me on my countless Berlin 'research trips'. These go way back to the 1980s when I lived in Berlin and had such fun exploring the city on both sides of the Wall with my family – Rod, Clare and Simon. Before the Wall fell in 1989, I managed to fit in several more visits including a ten day study tour to communist East Berlin. This was an unforgettable experience shared with fellow students on a Masters course in Contemporary German Studies.

After reunification, there were many school trips with colleagues and pupils from Hampton School in London. This meant that I was able to follow the rebirth of Berlin in great company and our partner school in Berlin, the Paul Natorp Schule in Schöneberg, always organised an excellent programme of visits. The former Head of English there, Dorothea Lehmann, has become a close friend and I owe her an enormous debt of gratitude for sharing her intimate knowledge of Berlin, her flat, and for helping so much with research.

For the past three years I have returned to Berlin for a few days each month, often with friends keen to find out what fires my passion for the city. They were all willing to help sample the sights, sounds and tastes of Berlin and stimulated ideas for the book. David Meggitt, Phil Carter, Catherine Goddard and Jean and John Noble donated photographs and Alice Jacobs and Peter Smith helped with editing. Insider tips were provided by several Berlin-based friends, including Timothey Ayers, Marly Barry, Eva Blumenschein, Adriana Grzanna, Maureen Metzger and James Woodhouse. Finally, I am immensely grateful to Johannes Jünemann, a Berliner with an incredible knowledge of the club and party scene, who wrote the 'Late Nightlife' chapter.

My sources are far too numerous to list in full and include books, websites and films in German, but among the best websites for English speakers visiting Berlin are the following:

www.berlin.de/international
www.berlin-hidden-places.com
www.berlin.unlike.net
www.exberliner.com
www.slowtravelberlin.com
www.spottedbylocals.com/berlin
www.visitberlin.de/en

The Author

Penny Croucher is an accomplished Germanist, writer and translator. She lived in Berlin in the 1980s and worked there as a journalist and tour guide. Her guide book to the divided city, "Berlin – An English Guide to Known and Unknown treasures", was published in 1987. Since then she has regularly returned to Berlin and closely observed its renaissance as the capital of reunified Germany. She taught German at a large London school, where she was Head of Modern Languages, and has led numerous school exchanges and visits to Berlin, enthusing hundreds of students with her passion for the city. She has also translated eleven books about Berlin from German into English.

Index of photographs

ArTo/Fotolia p. 27; Astra Kulturhaus p. 137; Berliner Prater Garten GmbH p. 148; Café Rix p. 155; Carter, Phil pp. 22, 59, 114, 117, 165, 178, 206; Croucher, Penny pp. 28, 37, 52, 73, 79, 84, 89, 91, 142, 147, 149, 169, 173, 205, 210; Erinnerungsstätte Notaufnahmelager Marienfelde (photographer: Andreas Tauber) p. 202; flashpics/Fotolia p. 174; Frannz Club p. 140; Friedrich, Marita p. 186; Friedrich, Uwe pp. 4, 6, 7, 8, 10, 11, 13, 16, 25, 30, 33, 38, 41, 42, 45, 47, 49, 50, 51, 57, 63, 74/75 (map), 76, 80, 82, 83, 87, 95, 97, 99, 100, 103, 105, 107, 108, 110, 111, 112, 113, 118, 119, 121, 123, 125, 152, 153, 157, 159, 160, 162, 171, 183, 185, 187, 190, 192, 193, 195, 199, 201, 208, 209, 212, 215, 217, 218, 219; Goddard, Catherine pp. 14, 197; Grüner Salon (photographer: Allie Carr) p. 141; Jünemann, Johannes pp. 130, 133; Kaffee Burger p. 136; Keller, Chris/bobsairport p. 139; Klein, David p. 188; Maats, Ralph/Fotolia p. 163; Martin-Gropius-Bau/jirka-jansch.com p. 69; Meggit, David pp. 20, 39, 46, 65, 181, 213; Noble, Jean and John pp. 204, 221; Palm, Peter pp. 18/19 (map); palomita0306/Fotolia p. 106; Publishers' archives pp. 17, 29, 34, 35, 55, 61, 67, 71, 85, 93, 126, 129, 189, 207; SO36/pro-kura nepp pp. 138; WARAS ARENA GmbH (photographer: Mike Breeuwer) p. 135; Wirtshaus Max und Moritz p. 151

Tandem Berlin   language courses
Learning German in small groups – We make you speak!

Tandem Berlin e.V.
Bötzowstraße 26   10407 Berlin (Prenzl. Berg)
tel. 030-4413003   Email: info@tandem-berlin.de
Public transport: Tram M4, Tram M10, Bus 200